Richard H. Wilmer, Helen H. Gardener

An Unofficial Patriot

Richard H. Wilmer, Helen H. Gardener
An Unofficial Patriot
ISBN/EAN: 9783337306618
Printed in Europe, USA, Canada, Australia, Japan
Cover: Foto ©Suzi / pixelio.de

More available books at **www.hansebooks.com**

AN UNOFFICIAL PATRIOT

BY

HELEN H. GARDENER

AUTHOR OF "IS THIS YOUR SON, MY LORD?" "PRAY YOU, SIR, WHOSE
DAUGHTER?" "PUSHED BY UNSEEN HANDS," "A THOUGHTLESS
YES," "MEN, WOMEN AND GODS," "FACTS AND FICTIONS
OF LIFE," ETC., ETC.

BOSTON
ARENA PUBLISHING COMPANY
COPLEY SQUARE
1894

Copyright, 1894,
by
HELEN H. GARDENER.
All rights reserved.

Arena Press

DEDICATION.

To those who, with heroic fortitude, have faced the questions involved; to whom was and is unknown the narrow vision which results in bitterness; who do not reckon upon great sociological problems in the evolution of the race as mere political capital; who are able at once to comprehend and to respect divergent opinion, and who do not brand as moral turpitude all that falls outside the scope of their own experience or preference; this volume is dedicated, in the hope that it may make plain some things that even the conscientious historian has failed to understand or record, and upon which literature is so far silent.

"Fame is the rose on a dead man's breast."

AN UNOFFICIAL PATRIOT.

CHAPTER I.

A SON OF VIRGINIA.

GRIFFITH DAVENPORT was a clergyman. I tell you this at the outset, so that you may be prepared to take sides with or against him, as is your trend and temperament. Perhaps, too, it is just as well for me to make another statement, which shall count in his favor or to his disadvantage, according to your own prejudices or convictions. He was a Southern man. He had been a slave-owner, and now he was neither the one nor the other. But in connection with, and in explanation of these last-mentioned facts, I may say that he had been a law-breaker in his native State, and was, at the very time of which I tell you, evading the law in the State of his adoption.

Both of these facts were the direct results of having been born to slave-ownership, and, at the same time, with a conscience which was of, and in harmony with, a different latitude and heredity. I trust that you will not infer from this last remark that I am of the opinion that the conscience of the Northern habitant is of more delicate fiber than is that of his Southern brother, who is of the same mental and social grade; for nothing could be farther from either the facts or my intentions herein. But that it is of a different type and trend is equally beyond controversy. The prickings of the one are as regular and as incessant, no doubt, as are those of the other; but the stimulating causes have different roots. Perhaps, too, it may sound strange to you to hear of one who can be spoken of as having a somewhat sensitive conscience and at the same time as being both a law-breaker and a law-evader. But certain it is, that with a less primitive conception of laws and of men, you will be able to adjust, to a nicety, the ideas therein conveyed, and also to realize how true it is that times, conditions, and environment sometimes determine the standard by which the rightfulness or wrongfulness of conduct is measured, and that it is quite within the possibilities for a man to be at once a law-breaker and a good man, or a law-keeper and a bad one.

But I am not intending to warp your judgment in advance, and you are to remember that whatever my opinion of the quality of the Rev. Griffith Davenport's conduct may be, there is another side to the matter, and that I shall not take it greatly to heart if you should find yourself on the other side.

But if, as I have sometimes heard readers say — who looked upon themselves as of a somewhat superior order — you do not take an interest in people who have placed themselves outside of the beaten pathway of legal regularity, it will be just as well for you to lay this little story aside now, for, as I have said, it is a story of a clergyman, a slave-holder, a law-breaker, and a law-evader, which, I admit, does not at the first blush present a picture to the mind of a person in whom you and I, my lofty and immaculate friend, would be greatly interested, or with whom we would care to associate for any protracted period. Still, I intend to tell the story, and in order to give you a perfectly clear idea of how all the more important events in this curiously complicated life came about, I shall be compelled to go back to the boyhood of young Davenport, so that you may catch a glimpse of the life and training, which were a prelude and a preparation—if you do not wish to look upon them as exactly a justification—of and for the later years of the life, which experienced such strange trials, complications and vicissitudes.

It was in the year eighteen hundred and twenty-four that the great sea of Methodism first began to beat with a force that was like that of a succession of mighty tidal waves upon the previously placid State of Virginia. Young Davenport had, at that time, just turned his fifteenth year, but it was not until nearly four years later, when the tide of interest and excitement had swept with a power and influence impossible to picture in these days of religious indifference and critical inquiry, into the homes and over the barriers of long-established things, that young Griffith's home felt the invasion to be a thing which it behooved gentlemen to consider seriously, or even to recognize as existing, if one may so express it, in an official sense.

As I suggested before, it would be difficult, in these later and less emotional days, when every school-boy knows of doubts and questionings in the minds of his elders, to picture adequately the serene lack of all such doubts and questionings in Griffith Davenport's boyhood.

To be sure there were, and, I venture to assume, always had been, disagreement and disputes over forms, methods, and meanings; but these were not fundamental doubts of fundamental beliefs, of which it would be entirely safe to say that young Davenport had never in his whole life heard one little doubt expressed or intimated, or that a question existed that could tend to make any one suspect that there were or could be unsettled realms in the system and plan of salvation as laid down by Christianity. He supposed, of course, that Christianity was an incontrovertible, fixed, and final religion. Different sects he knew there were, but all of these accepted the basic principle of Christianity. All sprang from the same root. Some grew eastward, some westward, and some made straight for heaven like the center shaft of a great oak; but each and all were true limbs of the same healthful trunk whose roots found anchorage in the bed-rock of eternal truth. He did not know that there were other trees quite as vigorous and even more expansive, each of which had sprung from the seed of human longing to solve the unsolvable. The "heathen" he had heard of, of course, in a condemnatory or pitying way, but he did not know or think of their worship as "religion." It was "fetichism," idolatry, superstition. Of Deists, he had heard, if at all, but vaguely; for it must be remembered that in the year of our blessed Lord eighteen hundred and twenty-seven the name of that famous Deist, Thomas Paine, who had done so much for the liberty and dignity of the great new nation, was not honored as it is to-day, and, indeed, so dense was the philosophical ignorance of that time, that the mention of the name of the author-hero of the Revolution was seldom made except in execration and contumely. Even of the Jews, from whom his religion came, Griffith had heard no good. They had slain the Christ, had they not? Their own God condemned the act, did he not?

Young Davenport supposed that this was all true. He also supposed that because of a blunder, made in ignorance and passion, in an age long past, a whole race had ever since been under the chastising hand of a just Jehovah, who had decreed that their humiliation and the expiation of the fatal blunder should be eternal. That there were Jews who were to-day good, devout and religious who still approved the attitude of Pilate toward the Christ, he did not know. He counted this class, therefore, as in some sort, Christians also. Mistaken in method, no doubt; superstitious and blundering perhaps; but still secretly filled with sorrow and shame for the awful crime of their race, and accepting the verdict of God and the disciplining punishment of time, he had no doubt of their final acceptance of what he believed established as eternal Truth, and their consequent redemption and salvation. The easy-going, gentle Episcopalianism of his home-training, with its morning and evening, perfunctory; family prayers, its " table grace " and its Sunday service, where all the leading families of the county were to be seen, and where the Rector read with so much finish and the choir sang so divinely, the same old hymns, week after week, had so far been as much a part of his life,—and were accepted as mechanically,—as were the daily meals, the unpaid negro labor, and the fact that his father, the old "Squire," sat in the best pew, because he had built and endowed the finest church in the State.

All these things had come to Griffith as quite a matter of course; as some equally important things have come to you and to me—and not at all as matters of surprise or as questions for argument.

That his father, the old major, swore roundly, from time to time, at the slaves, did not appeal to the boy's mind as either strange or reprehensible; so true is it that those things which come to us gradually, and in the regular order of events, do not arouse within us doubts and questionings as do sudden or startling additions to our development or intellectual equipment, when thrust unexpectedly in upon our ordinary surroundings. Such moral or social questions as were involved in the ownership of slaves had, up to that time, produced no more mental qualms in the boy than have the same questions as to ownership of lands or of horses upon you or me at the present time.

Jerry had been Griffith's own particular "boy" ever since he could remember, and, although Jerry was the older of the two, it would be wholly unfair to all parties concerned not to state clearly and fully that the righteousness and inevitability of the relationship of owned and owner, had no more sinister meaning for Jerry than it had for his young "Mos' Grif." So prone are we all to accept as a finality that to which custom has inured us.

Was Jerry an Episcopalian? Most assuredly! Were not all of the Davenports members of the established order in all things? And was not Jerry a Davenport? Not one negro on the whole plantation had ever for one little moment thought of himself as other than an Episcopalian,—in so far as the Almighty would permit one whose skin was black to be of the elect. They one and all felt a real and eager pride in the social and religious status of the Davenports, and had never even harbored a doubt that they would be permitted to polish the harps and hold the horses of that fortunate family when all should again be reunited in that better world, where all might be free but not equal—for "as one star differed from another," etc. No different dreams had ever, so far, visited master or slave.

"I could never be happy in heaven without Jerry," had settled the question in Griffith's mind, for of course his own destination was sure. And the negro felt equally secure when he thought, "Mos' Grif ain't gwine ter go nowhah widout me. Nobody else ain't gwine ter take cahr ob him. Nobody else know how."

But the unsettling times which brought Methodism, in a great and overwhelming wave, into the ranks of established things, brought also mutterings and perplexities and awakenings of another sort. Aroused energies, stimulated consciences, excited mentalities are ever likely to find varying outlets. Progressive movements seldom travel singly, and so it came about that, mingled with the new religious unrest, there were other and, perhaps you will say, graver questions so inextricably joined, in some minds that the one appeared to be the root and cause of the other.

"Is slavery right? If it is right for the laity, at least, is it not wrong for one who is an apostle of the Son of God, who had not where to lay His head? Should black men be free men?" and all the disturbing horde of questions which followed in the train of the new religion, began to float, at first in intangible ways, in the air. A little later they took form in scowl or hasty word, and at last crept into sermons, social discussions and legislative deliberations, as by degrees the echo of these latter floated down from Washington or filtered through other sources, from the Border States, where the irrepressible conflict had arisen in a new form to vex the souls and arouse the passions of men. The pressing question of free soil or slave extension had already begun to urge itself upon the public mind and to harass the Border States, finding utterance for or against that Congressional measure known as the Missouri Compromise Bill. Young Griffith Davenport had spent his seventeen years in an atmosphere of scholarly investigation and calm, where little of even the echoes of these disturbing influences had come. His home was a comfortable one—indeed, the finest in all that part of the "valley"; the library quite unusual in extent and quality for the time and place. Grif's tutor was a University man, his pleasures those of a country 'squire; for in Virginia, as in England, the office of "esquire," or justice of the peace, was wont to pass from father to eldest son, in families of consideration; and, indeed, at that early age Grif's father had, by degrees, turned the duties of the office over to the boy, until now no one expected to consult the "old 'squire" upon any ordinary topic. The "young 'squire" settled it, whether it were a dispute over dog-slain sheep or a misunderstanding about the road tax.

Upon this placid, "established" finality of existence it was, then, which descended a cyclone. Formalism in religion had run its course. The protest was swift, impassioned, sincere. Vigorous, earnest, but often unlearned men sprang into prominence at a single bound. Arguments arose. Men began to ask if the Almighty was pleased with forms in which the soul was dead—if mere words, and not sincere emotion of the heart, gratified God. Was it worship to simply read or repeat the words of another? Must not one's own soul, mind and heart furnish the key, as well as the medium, to aid in real devotion? Had the letter killed the spirit?

Young Griffith heard. The ideas fascinated him. Oaths from his father's lips struck him with a new meaning and a different force. Whereas they had been mere vocal emphasis, now they were fearful maledictions—and from a leading Christian, *the* leading Christian of the county!

Griffith pondered, trembled, listened again to the new religious teachers—to whose meetings he had, at first, gone in a spirit of mild fun, not in the least reprobated by his father—and had, at last, tremblingly, passionately believed.

CHAPTER II.

"I paint him in character." — *Shakespeare.*

THAT a Davenport should seriously contemplate leaving the "Mother Church," as the devotees of the Anglican establishment were given to calling their branch of the real Roman mother, was a proposition too absurd to be considered; and the old Major met his son's first suggestions, wherein this tendency was indicated, as the mere vaporings of a restless, unformed boy. He laughed loudly, guyed his son openly, and inquired jocosely which one of the pretty Methodist girls had struck his fancy.

"If it turns out to be serious, Grif, and you marry her, she will, as a matter of course, transfer her membership to the Mother Church. A true wife always follows her husband in all things. 'Thy people shall be my people, and thy God my God,' you know, Grif. Good old saying. Bible truth, my son. But who is the happy girl, you young scamp? There is rather a paucity of thoroughbreds among the Methodists, as they call this new craze. Don't make *that* kind of a mistake, my boy, whatever else you do. Better keep inside the paddock."

The old Major chuckled, and, turning on his heel, left his son covered with confusion, and with a sense of impotent zeal and conviction to which he could not or dared not give voice.

That this question of a truer, warmer, more personally stirring religious life did not touch a single responsive chord in the Major's nature, filled the son, anew, with misgivings. At first, these questionings led him to doubt himself, and to wonder if it could, after all, be possible that his own youth, inexperience and provincialism might really not lie at the root of his new unrest. He went to the Methodist meetings with a fresh determination to be serenely critical, and not to yield to the onrush of emotion which had grown so strong within him as he had listened, in the past, to the passionate and often ruggedly eloquent appeals of the pioneers of the new faith—or, perhaps, it were better to say, to the new expression of the old faith.

He gave up his extra Latin lessons, which had been his delight and the pride of his tutor and of his family, that he might have these hours for the study of the Bible and the few other books carried by the colporteurs or the circuit riders, who were beginning to overrun the State.

The old Major disapproved, but it was not his way to discuss matters with his family; and it may be doubted, indeed, if the Major grasped the significance and force of the tide which had overtaken his son, as it had rushed with the power of a flood over his beloved Virginia and left in its wake a tremendous unrest, and carried before it many of the most sincere and forceful characters and questions. Beyond a few twittings and an occasional growl, therefore, the old Major had ignored his son's gradual withdrawal from the ancient forms and functions and the fact that almost every Sunday morning, of late, had found the boy absent from the family pew and present two miles up the valley at the little log meeting-house of the Methodists. He was unprepared, therefore, to face the question seriously, when finally told by the boy's mother that Grif had decided that on his nineteenth birthday he would be baptized, and that he intended to enter the ministry as a circuit rider.

The joke struck the Major as good above the average. He laughed long and loud. He chuckled within himself all day. When evening came and Griffith appeared at the table the Major was too full of mirth and derision to content himself with his usual banter.

"Your mothah inforhms me," he began with the ironical touch in his tone held well under the sparkle of humor. "Your mothah inforhms me that to-morrow is your nineteenth birthday, you long-legged young gosling, and that you contemplate celebrating it by transmuting yourself into a Methodist ass with leather lungs and the manners, sir,—and the habits, sir, of—of—of a damned Yankee!"

As the Major had halted for words and the picture of his son as a circuit rider arose before him as a reality and not as a joke, his ire had gotten the better of his humor. The picture he had conjured up in his own mind of this son of his in the new social relations sure to result from the contemplated change of faith swamped the old Major's sense of the absurdity of the situation in a sudden feeling of indignation and chagrin, and the sound of his own unusual words did the rest.

Griffith looked up at his father in blank surprise. His mother said, gently, "Majah! Majah!" But the old 'squire's sudden plunge into anger had him in its grip. He grew more and more excited as his own words stirred him.

"Yes, sir, like a damned northern tackey that comes down here amongst respectable people to talk to niggers, and preach, as they call their ranting, to the white trash that never owned a nigger in their whole worthless lives, and tell 'em about the 'unrighteousness' of slavery! Why don't they read their Bibles if they know enough to read? *It* teaches slavery plain enough—'Servants obey your masters in all things,' and 'If a man sell his servant,' and 'His servant is his money,' and a good many more! Why don't they read their Bibles, I say, and shout if they want to, and attend to their own business? Nobody wants their long noses down here amongst reputable people, sowing seeds of riot and rebellion among the niggers!" The Major had forgotten his original point but it came back to him as Grif began to speak.

"But, sir——"

"But, sir!" he said, rising from his chair in his excitement, "don't 'but, sir,' me! I'm disgusted and ashamed, sir! Ashamed from the bottom of my hawt, that a son of mine—a Davenport—could for one moment contemplate this infernal piece of folly! A circuit rider, indeed! A damned disturber of niggers! A man with no traditions! Shouting and having fits and leading weak-minded women and girls, and weaker-minded boys and niggers into unpardonable, disgraceful antics and calling it religion! Actually having the effrontery to call it religion! It's nothing but infernal rascality in half the cases and pitiable insanity in the other half, and if I'd been doing my duty as a 'squire I'd have taken the whole pestiferous lot up and put one set in jail and the other set in an asylum, long ago! Look at 'em! Ducking 'converts,' as they call their dupes, in the creek! Perfectly disgraceful, sir! I forbid you to go about their meetings again, sir! Yes, sir, once and for all, I forbid it!"

The Major brought his fist down on the table with a bang that set the fine china rattling and added the last straw of astonishment and discomfort to the unusual family jar; for few indeed had ever been the occasions upon which even a mild degree of paternal authority had not been so quickly followed by ready and willing compliance that an outbreak of anything like real temper or authoritative command—other than at or toward the slaves—had been hardly within Grif's memory.

The boy arose, trembling and pale, and leaving his untouched plate of choice food before him turned to leave the room.

"Come back here, sir!" commanded the old Major. "Take your seat, sir, and eat your supper, sir, and——"

Mrs. Davenport burst into tears. The boy hesitated, parted his lips as if to speak, looked at his mother, and with a sudden movement of his hand toward a little book which he always carried these later days in his breast-pocket, he stepped to his mother's side. There was a great lump in his throat. He was struggling for mastery of himself but his voice broke into a sob as he said :

"'He that loveth father or mother more than Me is not worthy of Me. And he that taketh not his cross and followeth after Me, is not worthy of Me.'" He kissed his mother's forehead and passed swiftly out of the room. His horse stood at the front gate waiting the usual evening canter. Griffith threw his long leg over the saddle, and said to Jerry, who stood holding the bridle of his own horse, ready to follow as was his custom : "I don't want you to-night, Jerry. Stay at home. Good-night," and rode away into the twilight.

It would be difficult to say just what Griffith's plan was. Indeed, it had all been so sudden and so out of the ordinary trend of his life, that there was a numb whirl of excitement, of pain and of blind impulse too fresh within him to permit of anything like consecutive thought. But, with Grif, as with most of us when the crises of our lives come, fate or chance or conditions have taken the reins to drive us. We are fond of saying—and while we are young we believe—that we decided thus or thus; that we converted that condition or this disaster into an opportunity and formed our lives upon such and such a model. All of which is—as a rule—mere fond self-gratulation. The fact is, although it may wound our pride to acknowledge it, that we followed the line of least resistance (all things being considered, our own natures included) and events did the rest. And so when Grif turned an angle in the road, two miles from home, and came suddenly upon the circuit rider, who was to baptize the new converts on the following day, and when Brother Prout took it for granted that Grif was on his way to the place of gathering in order to be present at the preliminary meeting, it seemed to Grif that he had originally started from home with that object in view. His thoughts began to center around that idea. The pain and shock of the home-quarrel, which he had simply started out to ride off, to think over, to prepare to meet on the morrow, gradually faded into a dull hurt, which made the phrases and quotations and exhortations of Brother Prout sound like friendly and personal utterances of soothing and of paternal advice, and so the two miles stretched into ten and the camp-ground was reached, and for Griffith, the die was cast.

CHAPTER III.

THE IRONY OF FATE.

It has been well said that the heresies of one generation are the orthodox standards of the next; and it is equally true that the great convulsive waves of emotion, belief, patriotic aspiration or progressive emulation of the leaders of thought of one age, for which they are martyred by the conventionally stupid majority, become the watchwords and uncontrovertible basis of belief for the succeeding generation of the respectably unthinking, and furnish afresh, alas! the means, the motives and the power for the crucifixion of the prophets and thinkers of the new cycle. Mediocrity is forever sure that nothing better or loftier is in store. Genius sees eternal progress in perpetual change.

Much of the doings and many of the sayings of the new religious sect seemed to the people about them full of heresy, dangerous in tendency, and, indeed, blasphemous in its enthusiasms and its belief in and effort for an intimate personal relationship with a prayer-answering and a praise-loving God. To Grif, Brother Prout's fervor and enthusiasm of expression, his prayers which seemed the friendly communications of one who in deed and in truth walked with his God, instead of the old, perfunctory, formal reading of set phrases arranged for special days, which had to be hunted up in a book and responded to by all in exactly the same words, and with the same utter want of personal feeling, to Grif, these fervid, passionate, sincere and simple appeals of the kind old enthusiast seemed like the very acme and climax of a faith which might, indeed, move mountains.

"Amen! amen!"

"Praise the Lord, O my soul!"

"Thanks be to Almighty God!" echoed along the banks of the river, the loved Opquan, that had been to Grif a friend and companion from his earliest boyhood. He had never stood by its banks without an onrush of feeling that had tended to burst into a song of joy! From his grandfather's front porch and from the windows of his own room at home he could see it winding through the rocky hills and struggling for its right to reach the sea. He had skipped pebbles on it and waded across it at low tide, and had stood in awe at its angry and impetuous swirl when the spring rains had swollen it to a torrent of irresistible force. It seemed to Grif now that its waters smiled at him, and his eyes filled with tears that were of happiness not unmixed with a tender pain and regret—regret for he knew not what.

"Joy to the world, the Lord has come!" rang out with a volume and an impassioned sincerity which gave no room for the critical ear of the musician nor for the carping brain of the skeptic, had either been there to hear. "Let earth receive her King!" The hills in the distance took up the melody, and it seemed to the overwrought nerves of the boy that nothing so beautiful in all the world had ever been seen or heard before. "Let every heart prepare Him room, and heaven and nature sing!" Ah, was not heaven and nature, indeed, singing the most glorious song the earth had ever heard or seen when she made this valley? When she built these mountains, and threaded that little river over the stones? Griffith was lost in an intoxication of soul and sense. He was looking across the valley to the old home. His hands were clenched until the nails were marking the palms, and his voice rang out so clear and true that the neighborhood boys touched each other and motioned toward the young fellow with almost a sense of envy. Neither cultured musician nor cynic was there, and the softness of the air lent charm to the simple exercises which some of the youths had come in a spirit of fun to deride. It was restful to the weary, stimulating to the sluggish and soothing to the unhappy. They were carried out of their narrow and monotonous lives. If Griffith's heart had been sore and in a condition to be soothed by the words and prayers of Father Prout, how much more were his nerves and emotions in that unstrung and vaguely wounded and impressionable state where physical change and reaction is easily mistaken for religious fervor or exaltation, how much more was he in that state where melody joined to nature's most profligate mood of beauty in scene leads captive the soul!

During the meeting which had followed his arrival at the camp-ground Grif had passed through that phase of physical reaction which meant to him a "leading of the spirit" and, as he stood now on the banks of his beloved river pouring out his young heart in the hymn of his boyish fancy, he no longer doubted that he had, indeed, been "called" to be a circuit rider and to cast his lot with the new order of religious enthusiasts. He looked now upon his previous doubts as temptations of the devil and put, once and for all, their whisperings behind him and accepted the new lot as heaven and God-sent and intended.

Father Prout gave to all of his converts a choice in the form of their baptism. Leaning, himself, toward immersion, he still held that sprinkling was sufficient and with a lingering memory of his father's fling at "ducking converts in the creek," Griffith had determined to be sprinkled; but, as the last echoes of the old hymn died away, he stepped to the bank and indicated that he would be immersed. As he arose from the water his face was radiant, and when he had removed his immersion robe his eyes filled with happy tears as his father rode up to the edge of the grounds and held out his arms to the boy.

"My son," he said tremulously, "my son, fohrgive me. I have been unhappy all night. I did not realize that I was swearing at *you* until your mothah told me. Come home, my boy, and your new friends will be welcome at Rock Hall. God bless you, my son, come home, your mothah is unhappy."

Mr. Lengthy Patterson, a long-legged, cadaverous mountaineer who had wended his way from the distant fastnesses of the high perched log cabin which he called home and wherein he ate and slept when he was not engaged in those same occupations out under the stars where night—during his hunting and fishing expeditions—chanced to overtake him, had been watching Grif all day. The boy's radiant face the past hour had fascinated him. In his absorption he had stepped so close to the old Major as he and Grif stood making ready for the homeward ride, that Mr. Davenport made an instinctive gesture of impatient disapproval which called the naturally deferential woodsman back to his normal mental state.

"It is Lengthy Patterson, father," said Griffith, with his ever-ready impulse to cover the confusion of the unlucky or ignorant who were intrusive without a knowledge of the fact until a recognition of disapproval made self-consciousness painful.

Mr. Davenport moved as if to make amends for his previous manner by an offer to shake hands with the mountaineer—an unheard-of proceeding on the 'Squire's part.

"Oh, it's Lengthy Patterson, is it? I beg your pahrdon, Mr. a—Lengthy. I did not recognize you at——"

The long legs had moved slowly away. He turned around, tilted his half rimless hat further on to the back of his head, in lieu of lifting it, and in a voice as evenly graded to one single note as is that of a flying loom, remarked, as he kept on his way:

"No excuse. Say nothin'. Few words comprehends the whole."

"What did that fellow say, Grif?" asked his father, as they mounted.

Griffith laughed rather hysterically. The reaction was coming.

"It's just a phrase he has, father. They say he never was known to say anything else; but I expect that is a joke. He's an honest fellow and a splendid woodsman. He knows every crack in the mountains, and is a perfect terror to rattlesnakes. Don't you remember? He is the fellow who saved the old Randolph house that time it took fire, and got the children out. They say when Mrs. Randolph went away up to his cabin to thank him, he remarked that 'a few words comprehended the whole,' and fled the mountain until he was sure she had gone. He appears to be afraid of the English language and of nothing else on earth."

There was a long silence. The old Major was turned half out of his saddle, as was a habit of his, to rest himself. The horses were taking their own gait. Presently they turned a curve in the road and Grif suddenly threw his arm across his father's shoulder and leaned far over toward him. "Kiss me, father," he said, and before the moisture had dried out of their eyes and the great lump left their throats, both laughed a little in that shame-faced fashion men have when, with each other, they have yielded to their natural and tender emotions. But both horses understood and broke into a steady lope, and the chasm was bridged.

"Dars Mos' Grif! Dars Mos' Grif an' ole Mos'!" exclaimed Jerry as he saw the two horsemen in the distance. "Dey comin', Mis' Sallie, dey is dat! Lawsy me, Mis' Sallie, dey want no uste fer yo' ter be skeered dat a way 'bout Mos' Grif. He's des dat staidy dat yo' c'd cahry wattah on he haid, let er 'lone Selim ain't gwine ter let no trouble come ter Mos' Grif. But I dus 'low dat 'e oughter a tuck dis chile erlong wid 'im ter look arter 'im, dough. Dat's a fack. I knows dat. Run inter de kitchen, Lippy Jane, an' tell yo' maw dat Mos' Grif an' ole Mos' mose heah, an' she better git dem dar chicken fixins all raidy quick as ebber she kin. Dey gwine ter be hongry, sho's yo' bohn, dey is dat."

Lippy Jane sped away on her errand with that degree of enthusiasm which sprang from a consciousness of bearing a welcome message to expectant listeners, when suddenly, as she passed a group of idle compeers, one of the boys flung upon her lower lip, where it lodged and dangled in squirming response to her every motion, a long yellow apple peeling. She did not pause in her onward course, but called back in belligerent tones at the offender:

"I des gwine ter lef dat erlone dar, now, an' show hit ter Mos' Grif! I is dat! You nasty little nigger!" and she reappeared, after giving her message in the kitchen, with the pendant peel still reposing upon the superfluous portion of the feature to which she was indebted for her name.

CHAPTER IV.

THE REV. GRIFFITH DAVENPORT.

So desirable a candidate was speedily ordained, and Brother Prout himself rode with the boy on his two first rounds of the not far-distant circuit which was soon to be placed in charge of this youth who had so suddenly taken on the duties, responsibilities and desires of a man. Grif's temperament had always been so merry and frank and full of the joyful side of life that he found himself at once ill at ease and hampered by the feeling that he must curb his spirits. Brother Prout, whose own nature was only less buoyant, patted Grif on the back and advised against the change which he clearly saw the boy was trying to compass.

"Don't grow dull, Brother Davenport," he said one day, as they were riding toward the home of one of their members to make a pastoral visit. "Don't grow dull and old before your time. Religion is joy, not gloom. Your message to these people is happiness. Let your bright young face and voice bear testimony for the Lord, and prove to them that all His ways are ways of pleasantness, and all His paths are paths of peace. Let your neighbors see that in forsaking your old life you have not lost the best and most glorious part of it. You take that with you in addition to the rest. Laugh with them that laugh, and weep with them that weep. I'm an old man, now, and I never did have your spirits; but we need just that in our labors, my son. Don't allow yourself to grow dull. With your nature you will win and not drive souls to the Lord."

Such advice cheered the boy and made him feel less strongly the great change in his life. The long hours of riding his fine horse over the roads and by-paths of his beloved and beautiful valley; the talks with friends or strangers who were never strangers for long, since mutual acquaintance or intermarriage had made of the whole state almost one family, proved attractive and interesting to him. He found in this new work a real and fresh happiness. Fording swollen streams, searching for obscure mountain passes, riding alone or with a chance companion through extensive stretches of woodland, listening to, and often answering the notes of birds or the cry of some animal, were congenial occupations to the young parson, and his form rounded out and his face gradually settled into mature but gentle and kindly lines, and it was now grown to be his invariable rule to compose his sermons as he rode. He never wrote them. Some text would fix itself in his mind as he read his little black Testament night or morning, and upon that text he would build a simple and kindly talk which reached and touched his handful of listeners as no elaboration of rhetoric could have done.

Some days he would ride along for miles, humming or singing a single tune, while a train of thought for his next sermon was building itself up in his mind. Selim, the fine young sorrel, knew quite well what to do, and fell into a walk or a gentle canter, according to the briskness or volume of the notes that rose over his back. If " How-tedious-and-tasteless-the-hours, when-Jesus-no-longer-I-see," trailed out softly, with long and undevised breaks in the continuity of sound and sense, Selim walked demurely, and saw no ghosts or interesting things whatsoever in woods or stream or distant valley. But when "Joy to the world! The Lord has come!" rang out, continuous and clear, Selim knew that he might even shy at a stone, and make believe a set state of terror at sight of a familiar old post or a startled groundhog; or that if he were to break into an unexpected gallop, no harm would be done, and that he would be pretty sure of some playful remarks and a bit of teasing from the rider, whose sermon, Selim knew full well, was finished. But so long as "Joy to the mm-mmmm-m-mmmm-mmm——Let earth mmmm—mmmmm-mmmher King," greeted his ears, Selim knew that the responsibility of ford or path rested with him, and many a ford did Selim take before his rider realized that he had come to it. If swimming were necessary, Selim struck out with a powerful stroke, and came up on the other bank with a proud stamp of his feet and a whinny that bid for the recognition of his prowess that he knew was sure to come to him.

"Whoa, old fellow! Stop and get your wind! Steady! That was a pretty stiff current, wasn't it? There, take a nibble! Been some pretty heavy rains around here, haven't there? But what do you and I care about rains and currents? Whoa, there, you rascal, keep your nose off my sleeve! O, you will, will you? Well, there, there, there, I've wiped it all off as good as ever. T-h-a-t's right; nip off some of these fresh buds. Here, let's take our bit out. Tastes better, doesn't it? Oh, you will, will you, old wet nose? Ha! ha! ha! Selim, you know more than most folks, you old humbug!"

If his master sat down and became absorbed in thought, or in his little black book, Selim would browse about for an hour; but at the first note of a hymn the faithful fellow came to have his bridle replaced, and was ready for a gallop or a walk, as his rider should indicate.

At first the young circuit rider would take a swollen ford, when a safer one could have been found a mile or two farther on, or he would ride miles out of his way to make a pass in the mountains, when, had he known the fact, an obscure but safe one was near at hand. But, as the years passed by, both Selim and his master would have scorned a guide, and, night or day, the country became to them like the fields of one's own estate, so familiar were they with it all. In this pass was a great nesting place, where, year after year, the circuit rider talked aloud to the birds, and fancied that they knew him. Many a friendly note of reply to his whistle or call gained a hearty laugh.

"Feel jokey to-day, do you, you ridiculous Bob White? Wish I could translate that into English. Know it was a good joke from the twist you gave it, but I'm no linguist. You'll have to excuse me if I don't reply intelligently," he would call out to some unusually individualized note, and Selim would whisk his tail in utter disapproval of a man who would so foolishly converse with birds—such little insignificant things as they were—when here was a full-grown, blooded horse, right under his nose! The pride and arrogance of species is great within us all—and Selim had associated much with man.

"Hello! Where's that great-grandfather of yours that I saw here the last time we crossed your ford?" Griffith remarked aloud to a frisky little trout, as it whisked past Selim's feet. "Hope nobody's caught him. Give him my regards when you get home."

Just then Selim's feet struck the bank, and, as he scrambled up, he shied a little, and his master recognized the long legs before him as those of the mountaineer in homespun trousers and hickory shirt, who had vexed the old Major at the baptizing in the Opequan that now seemed so long ago.

"Good-morning——" began the young minister, when Lengthy's gun went suddenly to his shoulder, there was a flash, a report. Selim sprang to one side, and the mountaineer poked with his gun where the horse had stood. "Look down. Say nothin'. Few words comprehend th' whole;" he remarked to the astonished circuit rider, as he held up on the end of his gun a still writhing, ugly, dying snake, which had been coiled to spring. He was too confused, or too mentally embryonic to do more than grin in gratified silence at the thanks and compliments from the young preacher: for it was somewhat infrequently that Lengthy was addressed by one of Griffith's type, and the very sincerity of his evident admiration for the circuit rider still farther handicapped his already abnormally developed awkwardness of manner. It is possible that the vocabulary of this swarthy mountaineer (whose six feet and seven inches of bone and sinew had fixed upon him the only name that Pastor Davenport had ever heard applied to him), it is possible, I say, that his vocabulary may have been fuller than it was generally supposed to be. Among his fellows it is just possible that he may have ventured upon language with more freedom; but certain it is that when Lengthy was in the presence of what he was pleased to call "quality," the limitations were painfully apparent, and there was a legend—which appeared to have as solid a basis as belongs to most—that whatever slight variations he might venture upon as an opening remark, the *finale*, if one may so express it, was sure to be the same.

Mr. Davenport asked after his health, that of his family, the neighborhood in general and finally, unable to extract anything beyond a nod or a single word from the giant who had pitched the still squirming rattlesnake from the end of his gun into the river, Griffith took another tack.

"River seems to be unusually high. Selim had all he could do, didn't you, old fellow? Been having a freshet here, haven't you?"

Lengthy pointed with his gun, to the remnants of a rail fence, now high on the bank, in the top rails of which clung half-dry weeds and river refuse.

"Look there. Few words comprehend th' whole."

Griffith smiled, gave up the task of conversing with his admirer, shook the bridle on Selim's neck and with a cheery "Well, I'm glad to have met you. Good-bye," rode on toward the village where he was soon to begin his first year's pastorate as a "located" preacher. As he rode along he almost regretted the change. These had been happy years to the simple-hearted, but ardent young fellow; but he was consoled when he saw before him in mental vision the home in which pretty, black-eyed Katherine LeRoy was to preside—for the young circuit rider had found his fate and, alas! it had not been inside the Episcopal paddock nor even in the Methodist fold—such pranks does Fate play with us, such liberties does Cupid take, even with the hearts of those whose mission it is to deal with other things! Very early in the new life Griffith had stayed one night at the hospitable home of Katherine's father. In spite of all, his heart was lonely and his face less bright than in the old days. Miss Katherine saw. Miss Katherine was kind—and Miss Katherine's sweet face traveled many a mile with the young preacher after he, as Selim was well aware, should have been humming a hymn and composing that sermon for the morrow. But Selim was discreet; and when he shook his head or whinnied or changed his gait and Griffith did not heed, Selim plodded demurely on and waited. But as the months had gone by and Selim had carried the young master up the same lane a few times and had observed the same silent abstraction after each visit, he had grown to know very well indeed that this was a marked house and that Griffith liked to go there. So it came to pass that after the dark eyes had traveled with the young preacher and peered over his shoulder into his Testament and interfered sadly with the trend of his thoughts on sacred things, it had grown to be very certain to Griffith that something would have to be done. Then it was that for the first time he thought how little he had to offer. Not even a home! Not even his own companionship! For all these six years he had traveled his different circuits and slept where he found himself as night came on, and preached here or there as he had been directed. His home had been literally in his saddle, and his salary had been too insignificant to mention. The old Major, who to a degree, had become reconciled to the new order of things, had at first insisted that Jerry follow and care for the young master; but Griffith had argued that it ill became one who had taken such a step to take with him a body servant, and it had almost broken Jerry's heart to be compelled to stay at the old home-place and allow young Mos' Grif to saddle and feed Selim, if need be, and care for and brush his own clothes. This latter had, indeed, led to the loss of most of his limited wardrobe, for he had left behind him, at the house of some " member" a piece of clothing or some toilet article very often, at the first; but as it never failed to be returned to him on his next round, the leather saddle-bags retained about the same proportions from month to month, replenished as they were by his mother and Jerry on his frequent visits home.

But it was when the thought of a wife and a home of his own first came to Griffith that the life of a circuit rider grew less attractive and he wondered if it would be right to ask to be " located " or " stationed " as some of the married men were. To be sure they must change their " station " year by year and so tear up the little roots they could strike in so brief a period, but at least it gave something like a home and a " charge" to the preacher, and he—not his family—was the sole subject of solicitude and consideration to the authorities who governed his movements. Had not the Lord said to those whom He sent forth to preach that they must go from place to place leaving behind all family ties? Had not He so lived? Had not Paul and Timothy and the twelve? Later on had it not been so with the many until wealth and love of ease and the things of this world undermined the true faith?

But human nature is strong, and all faiths in the past have—as all in the future will continue to do—accommodated themselves to the human needs and demands of those who sustain the theory as infallible, immutable, unchangeable and unchanging; but modify it to fit the times, the natures and the conditions in which they strike root. If Mohammed will not go to the mountain, the mountain will come to Mohammed.

So when the young circuit rider had stopped again, as had grown to be his habit, with the family of Katherine LeRoy, and when she, with quaint coquetry, had met his equally quaint courtship by finally accepting him on condition that he "take a charge" he had asked the presiding elder to locate him as a married man for the next year since he was about to marry. Brother Prout had approved, and the matter had been settled with little difficulty.

The courtship was unique. The young parson had grown to be so great a favorite wherever he went that his cheerfulness, his kindly, simple and sincere nature insured him hearty welcome even outside of his own flock. His superior birth and breeding made him a marked man within his denomination. Many were the speculations as to which rosy-cheeked Methodist girl he would find nearest his ideal, and jokes were many at the expense of this or that one if he but stopped twice at her father's house.

At last it became plain that in one neighborhood he preferred to stay overnight with the family of Bernard LeRoy, a staunch and uncompromising Presbyterian, and it did not take long for others to discover why; but so sure was Mr. LeRoy, himself, that it was to his own superiority to his neighbors that the visits were due, that the times when a few words alone with Miss Katherine were possible were few indeed. The large, ready, hearty hospitality of the time and of Virginia were exemplified in this household. All welcomed him. Old, young, white and black alike; and the wide porch or great rooms and halls gave space and hearty invitation to family and neighborly gatherings. So it came about that at last Griffith felt that he could wait no longer. He must know his fate. The demure Katherine had reduced him to a mere spirit of unrest in spite of the presence of others, and while all sat talking of crops, politics, religion, neighborhood happenings, rains, swollen streams and the recent freaks of lightning, the young minister took from his pocket the little black Testament and drew a line around the words, " Wilt thou go with this man?" and handing it to Miss Katherine he asked: " Will you read and answer that question for me, Miss Katherine?" Their eyes met, and although Griffith returned to his seat and essayed to go on with the conversation with her father, they both understood.

Her dark eyes ran over the words, her color rose and fell, but, contrary to the hope of the young preacher, she did not mark and return the reply. She carelessly turned the leaves and his heart sank. He gave abstracted replies to her father and twice failed to hear what was said, and still Miss Katherine turned the leaves. At last he believed that she had either not understood or that she did not intend to reply, and with a sinking heart he rose to go. Selim had been put away. The circuit rider was always expected to stay overnight. He explained in a vague way that this time it would be best for him to go to a Methodist neighbor's two miles farther on. Was it that reply which decided dark-eyed Katherine not to farther tease her lover? Did she fear the wiles of the plump, demure girl in the quaint, unribboned bonnet who looked such open admiration into the eyes of the young preacher. However that may be, certain it is that at this juncture and under cover of the general movement to send for the guest's horse, Miss Katherine took from her belt a pansy and putting it between the pages to mark where she had drawn a line, she gave the little book back to its owner. He saw the movement and glanced within: " Why have I found grace in thine eyes that thou shouldst take knowledge of me—seeing I am a stranger?" He read and his heart leaped. "A stranger!" She was not of his fold! It was *that* she thought of! He looked at her and both understood. He could ride away now and both would be content, even though he were under the roof with the quaint little Methodist bonnet.

As they moved toward the door the two young people managed to pass out alone and Griffith took her in his arms for one brief instant and kissed her lips.

"Thank God!" he whispered. "Thank God, for this last and holiest blessing! I love you next to my Saviour, Katherine. Sometimes I pray it may not be more than I love Him."

She laughed, a soft little ripple, and drew back just as her father appeared at the door.

"I shall not pray that," she said, as he mounted, and the young preacher rode away into the darkness with no disapproval of the heresy upon his radiant face. Selim knew that this was a strange proceeding—this late departure—and he shook his head so violently that the buckles of his bridle rattled. The young minister made no sign, but when, a little farther on, there suddenly arose over his back, the notes of a long-forgotten song, Selim cast one eye backward and started at the break-neck pace of his youth.

"The moon is beaming brightly, love,
  Te tum te tum te te!
A trusty crew is waiting, love,
  Away, away with me!"

Selim's surprise knew no bounds. He had not heard that song since before the day his young master went, for some strange reason, into the Opquan river, with Brother Prout. Something unusual had happened, that was very clear. Something that carried the young preacher quite out of himself and into a world where sermons and hymns were not; and, although the song was gay, Selim felt a tug at his bridle that meant a slower pace.

"Yea! old fellow, y-e-a!" Selim was surprised again. He stopped short.

"G'ap! g'lang!

"Far o'er the deep, o'er the deep, o'er the d-e-e-e-p,
  Far o'er the deep blue sea!
Far o'er the deep, o'er the deep, o'er the d-e-e-e-p,
  Far o'er the deep blue sea!
Oh, come and share a sailor's heart—far o'er the deep
  blue sea!"

Perhaps Selim was not exactly scandalized, but he felt that it would not be judicious to reach the home of the quaint Methodist bonnet too prematurely. And Selim walked.

CHAPTER V.

A MAN'S CONSCIENCE.

But all this was away back in the years when you and I were not born, my friend, and, therefore, the only reason I tell you about it or expect you to be interested in such simple and far-off lives is that you may know something of the early habits and surroundings of the man who, I began by warning you, became a law-breaker; for, I hold it to be a self-evident fact that however true it is that heredity stamps the character with its basic principles and qualities, it is never wise to forget that it is to environment, circumstance and education that we owe its modifications and the direction of its final development. But now that you will be able to picture to yourself the man as he then was, and his surroundings and conditions, I will tell you as directly as I can the story of his offense; but first I must explain that when his coming marriage to Miss Katherine LeRoy was announced at his home, the old Major objected again, but this time more mildly, to the choice his son had made.

"Her people are good, wholesome, respectable folks, my son," he said ; "but—but, Grif, why couldn't you have found a girl of—well, one of the families you were brought up with. Mind, boy, I'm not saying anything against Miss Katherine. I've heard—and I don't doubt it—that she is a mighty nice sort of a girl; but——"

The Major had grown milder in his methods with his son, and he hesitated to speak words which might cause pain hereafter.

"Of course, Grif," he went, on after an awkward pause, "of course, if you love each other—and—and—well, if the thing is settled, I have only to congratulate you, and to say that I am truly glad to have you settle down, so I'll be able to know where you are. It's deucedly disagreeable not to know from week to week where to put a finger on you—such a tacky sort of shifty sensation about it. I can know now at least a year at a time. Perfectly ridiculous custom it is to move a preacher just when he gets acquainted with the people, and they begin to trust him! Infernal habit! I'd as soon live on a boat and just anchor from time to time in another stream and call it home—and—and living. I've come to respect your sincerity, Grif, but I can't respect the sense of a denomination that has no idea of the absolute value of stability, of continuity of association, between its pastor and its people. Why, just look at the thing! It uproots the best sentiments in both, and makes a wanderer of one who ought to be, not only by precept, but by example, stable and faithful and continuously true to those who look up to him. Why, a scamp can pose for a year or two as a saint; but it takes real value to live a lifetime in a community and be an inspiration and a guide to your members. Then just look at it! Nobody who has any self-respect is going to talk of his inner life to a stranger! We are all alike in that. We pose and pretend and keep our shutters up, mentally and morally, with a new-comer. Gad! I can't see the wisdom nor the sense of any such rules."

"Has its good points, father," said Grif, whose quiet chuckle from time to time had stirred the Major to unusual earnestness. He wanted to get at his son's real views on the subject. "Has some redeeming qualities, after all, father, quite aside from the Bible teaching upon which the leaders of our church base it. There are men—even ministers, I'm afraid, whom one enjoys much better when they are on another circuit; and I may as well confess to you that there are circuits a man enjoys a good deal better when he's not on them—after he has left."

"Some of the old boy in you yet, Grif," laughed the Major, slapping his son on the back. "Better not say that to Father Prout, or he will keep you on one of that kind for discipline."

Jerry was filled with delight when told of the coming marriage of Mos' Grif. Jerry's own wife had long since presented him with twins, and it was his delight to show off the antics of these small ebony creatures to Griffith whenever he was at home. It was at first arranged that this family only should go to form the new household.

The mutterings born in a different clime and under other conditions had now reached proportions which could not be wholly ignored. In many a long ride over the mountain or valley paths in the past few years had Griffith pondered the question, and he had definitely decided in his own mind that for one who had cast his lot with the itinerant Methodist clergy, at least, the ownership of slaves was wrong. He would never buy nor sell a human being. Upon that point his mind was clearly and unalterably made up. But Jerry and his family were to be a part of the new household while yet they remained, as before, the old Major's property. To this Griffith had consented readily, for Miss Katherine must have an efficient cook and Jerry would be of infinite use. Griffith had drawn a picture of a small house in the village in which this beautiful dream of his was to be realized; but, as the time drew near, the old Major developed his own plans with such skill as to carry his point.

When the house was to be looked for he said: "See here, Grif, you are a good deal younger than I am, and some of the older slaves are pretty hard to manage. They can't work a great deal, and they get into mischief one way and another. Look at that set over in the end cabin—they always did like you best—and since you have been gone so much they are a good deal of trouble to me. They've got to be cared for somehow. I wish you'd take them. They can do a lot of useful things if they are away from the others, and you can get twice as much work out of them as I can. They are stubborn with me, and it wears my soul out to deal with 'em. I've needed your help a good many times since you've been away, but I did not like to say much. I think, now you are going to settle down, that you ought to think of your father's needs a little, too."

Grif winced. He recalled that he had always pushed his father's problem aside in his thoughts when he had settled or solved his own. He realized how unfair that was. He felt the force of the Major's complaint.

"Of course, I'll do anything I can, father, to help you; but I can't take a lot of negroes to a village and——"

"That's just it! Just it, exactly! Of course you can't. I didn't intend to ask you just yet, but I want you to give up that foolish idea of taking Katherine to town to live. She can't stand it. You are asking enough of a woman, God knows, to ask her to put up with your sort of life anyhow, let alone asking a girl that has been respectably brought up on a plantation to give all that up and go to a miserable little village. It is not decent to live that way! Cooped up with a lot of other folks in a string of narrow streets! I'd a good deal rather go to jail and done with it. Now, what I want and what I need you to do, is to take that other plantation—the one down on the river—your grandfather's place—and take some of the hands down there and you can let them work the place. How in the name of thunder do you suppose you and Katherine are going to live on your ridiculous salary? Salary! It isn't enough to dignify by the name of wages—let alone salary! Y' can't live on it to save your lives. Katherine can't——"

"But, father——"

"That farm down there is plenty near enough

to town for you to ride in every single day if you want to and—look here, boy, don't you think you owe a little something to your father? I'm getting old. You don't begin to realize how hard it is on me to meet all these difficulties that other men's sons help them with."

The Major had struck that chord with full realization of its probable effect, and he watched with keen relish the troubled and shamed look on the face before him. Griffith made a movement to speak, but the Major checked him with a wave of the hand.

"That farm is just going to wreck and ruin, and I haven't the strength to attend to that and this both. Besides, these negroes have got to be looked after better. Pete is growing more and more sullen every year, and Lippy Jane's temper is getting to be a holy terror. She and Pete nearly kill each other at times. They had a three-cornered fight with Bradley's mulatto, Ned, the other day, and nearly disabled him. Bradley complained, of course. Now, just suppose Ned dies and Bradley sues me? It seems to me it is pretty hard lines when a man has a son and——"

"But, father——"

"Now, look here, Grif, don't 'but' me any more. I've had that house on the other place all put in order and the negro quarters fixed up. The negroes can belong to me, of course, if you still have that silly idea in your head about not wanting to own them, but you have got to help me with them or——Then damn it all, Grif, I don't intend it to be said that a daughter-in-law of *mine* has to live in a nasty little rented house without so much as a garden patch to it. It is simply disgraceful for you to ask her to do it! I——"

"Father, father!" said Grif, with his voice trembling; "I—you are always so good to me, but I—I——"

The old Major looked over his glasses at his son. Each understood, and each feigned that he did not. The Major assumed wrath to hide his emotion. "Now, look here, Grif, I don't want to hear anything more about this business! You make me mad! Who am I to go to for help in managing my land and my niggers if I can't depend on you for a single thing? That's the question. Confound it all! I'm tired out, I tell you, looking after the lazy lot, and now you can take your share of the work. What am I going to do with the gang if I've got to watch 'em night and day, to see that they are kept busy enough not to get into trouble with each other, and get me in trouble with my neighbors. Just suppose Pete had killed Bradley's Ned, then what? Why, I'd have been sued for a $1,000 and Pete would have been hung besides! I tell you, boy, I'm too old for all this worry, and I think it's about time I had a little help from you. I——"

The young preacher winced again under the argument, although he knew that in part, at least, it was made for a purpose other than the one on the surface. In part he knew it was true. He knew that his father had found the task heavy and irksome. He knew that the negroes preferred his own rule, and that they were happier and more tractable with him than with the old 'Squire. He knew that as the times had grown more and more unsettled and unsettling, his father had twice had recourse to a hired overseer and that the results had been disastrous for all. He knew that other sons took much of this care and responsibility from the aging shoulders of their fathers. He hesitated—and was lost. He would take the negroes with him and live on the other place—at least one year!

But when Miss Katherine brought with her her father's gift of slaves—which Mr. LeRoy had tried hard to make sufficiently numerous to impress the old Major—Grif, to his dismay, found himself overseer and practically the owner of twenty-two negroes—and he on a salary of $200 per year! With a plantation to work, the matter of salary was, of course, of minor importance. But Griffith had not failed to see glimpses of a not far-distant future, in these past few years as he had read or heard the urgent questions of political policy which had now become so insistent in the newer border states—a future in which this life must be changed. Riots and bloodshed, he knew, had followed in the train of argument and legislative action. Slaves had run away and been tracked and returned to angry masters. But the basic question as to whether it was right for man to hold property in man had, so far, been presented to his mind in the form of a religious scruple and with a merely personal application. *Should ministers of his Church* buy and sell black men? Griffith had definitely settled in his own mind that they should not. But whether they should inherit or acquire by marriage such property, had, until now, hardly presented a serious face to him. And now, in the form in which they came to him, he saw no present way out of the difficulty even had he greatly desired it.

I have no doubt that to you, my friend, who were not born in these troublous times, and to you, my neighbor, who lived in another latitude, the problem looks simple enough. "He could free the slaves which were in his power," will be your first thought. "I would have done that," is your next, and yet it is dollars to doughnuts that you would have done nothing of the kind. Oh, no! I am not reflecting upon your integrity, nor your parsimony—although I have not observed any tendency you may have toward dispensing with your property by gift— but to other and more complicated and complicating questions with which you would have found yourself surrounded, and with which your private inclinations would have come into violent collision, as Griffith Davenport discovered; and surely, my friend, you would not care to be written up in future years as a violator of the law—you who value so lightly "that class of people" that you have often said, quite openly, that you cared very little to even read about them, and deplored the fact that writers *would* thrust them into respectable literature!

Griffith had watched the coming storm in the southwest. He had hoped and prayed (and until now he had believed) that for himself, at least, the question was settled. He would never own slaves, therefore he would not be called upon to bear any personal part in the coming struggle. But a wife's property was a husband's property in Virginia, in those far-off barbaric days, and so Griffith found himself in an anomalous position, before he knew it, for Mr. LeRoy had given Katherine her slaves as a marriage portion, and had striven to make sure that their number and quality should do honor to the daughter-in-law of her prospective husband's father. Mr. LeRoy had an exalted opinion of the position and importance of the old Major—

or as he always called him, of "old 'Squiah Davenpoaht."

But so matters stood until, a few years later, an accident happened, which resulted in the death of the old Major. When the will was opened, Griffith found himself forced to confront the question of ownership of slaves, fairly if not fully. The will left "to my beloved son, Griffith, all the slaves now living with him, together with the farm upon which he now lives and the old homestead; with the admonition that he care for and protect the old slaves and train and employ the young." His other property was devised in accordance with his wishes, leaving to his grandchildren and distant relatives the other slaves and live stock.

Meantime, as this would indicate, there had been born to Griffith several children—three boys and a little baby girl—which now filled the hearts and home with life and joy.

The exigencies of his ministerial life had so far made it necessary for him to leave the plantation but twice. Father Prout had managed to have his "stations" rotate from one small town to another in the immediate vicinity, and, with his growing stoutness, Mr. Davenport had taken to driving, chiefly, since Selim had been retired from active service, to and from his places of meeting week after week. Twice, for a year each time, he had been compelled to leave the plantation in charge of Jerry and remove to a more distant town, where the small house and unaccustomed conditions had resulted in ill health for Katherine and the children. But now they were on the "place" again and were owners of much that required that they face larger and more complicated responsibilities—and what was to be done? Griffith had made up his mind, definitely, that he did not want his sons to grow up in a slave-owning atmosphere. He had read and thought much of the struggle over the Missouri Compromise Bill. He had hoped great things from it, and had beheld its final repeal with dismay. He had seen, so he believed, in it the arm that was destined to check if not to wipe out human slavery. How this was to be done he did not know; but that he hoped for it, for all men, he knew. For himself he was quite sure that as a preacher, if not as a man, it was wrong. He had determined to so educate his sons that they would not blame him for shutting them out from at least the inherited possibilities of the institution which had fallen upon him. But now, what could be done? The Major's will had thrown the task definitely upon him and had greatly increased the difficulties. He knew that it was against the laws of his state to free the negroes and leave them within its borders. Exactly what the terms of the law were, he did not know; but it was easy to realize its need and force. Free negroes were at once a menace to all parties concerned, both white and black. They had no work, no homes, no ties of restraint and responsibility. They were amenable to no one and no one was their friend. They could starve, or they could steal, or they could go North. If they did the first—in a land of plenty—they were not made of that stuff out of which human nature is fashioned, be that nature encased in a white or in a black skin. If they did the second they fared far worse than slaves—the chain-gang for home and the law for a driver has horrors worse than even slavery—at least so thought the colored man of 1852. But if they attempted to achieve the last of the three alternatives their lot was hardest of all. They must leave home, family, wife, children, parents and friends—all that made life endurable to a patient, affectionate, simple nature—and find what? Neither friends, welcome nor work! A climate in which they suffered, a people amongst whom their rarity and the strangeness of their speech and color made of them objects of curiosity and aversion —where the very children fled from them in fright—little children like those whom they had nursed and fondled and who always had loved them! They would find the prejudice against their color intense beyond belief, for few indeed were the men or women in the free states who would give work of any kind to these strange-looking and stranger-speaking creatures. Indeed, no one was more shocked to learn than was Griffith, that in some of the border states it was illegal to give employment to these ex-slaves. All this Griffith was destined to learn to his cost. He knew, already, that slaves trained as his father's were, had no conception of hard and constant work such as was demanded of the northern laborer. He knew that they could not hope to compete with white workmen in a far-away field of labor even could they get the work to do. He knew that they would be the sport—where they were not the game and victims—of those white laborers. He knew that the employer (were they so fortunate as to find one) would not be slow to learn that they accomplished less and ate more than did their white rivals. That alone would, of course, settle their chances of competition, and starvation or crime would again become their only alternative.

A freed slave, in a country where slavery still existed, was a sorry and unhappy spectacle; but a freed slave in competition with freemen was a tragedy in black!

Griffith had fought his battle alone. It is true that he had talked much with his wife on the subject, and it is also true that her faith in and love for him made her ready acquiescence in his final decision a matter of course; but with no outlook into the political world, with no mental scope beyond the horizon prescribed as suitable for women, she could give him nothing but loyalty. She could echo his sentiments. She could not stimulate or aid his thought. Attuned to follow, she could not lead, and was equally unfitted to keep even step with him side by side. She did not share, nor could she understand, her husband's acute mental misgivings and forebodings. The few times she had spoken to her father of them, he had said that she need not worry. "Griffith is no fool. He'll get over this idiotic notion before long. It is reading those damned Yankee speeches that is the trouble with him. You just be patient. He'll get over it. The old 'Squire knew how to cure him. Like to know what he'd do with all those niggers? But Griffith is no fool, I tell you, if he is a Methodist." Katherine had not relished the last remark, and she did not believe that her father quite comprehended how deep a hold on Griffith the idea of freedom for the blacks—and freedom from ownership of them for himself—had taken; but she was silenced.

CHAPTER VI.

"My conscience whispers."—*Shakespeare.*

But at last the crisis came. One of the girls—Sallie, a faithful creature—had married "Bradley's John," and now John was about to be sold and sent to Georgia. Either John must be separated from his wife and child, or Sallie must be sold, or Mr. Davenport must buy John and keep him here! The final issue had come! John begged to be bought. Sallie pleaded not to be allowed to be sold, nor to be separated from her husband. Katherine agreed to plead for Sallie, who had been her own playmate ever since she could remember.

"Git Mos' Grif ter buy John, Mis' Kate! Fo' God's sake, Mis' Kate, git 'im ter buy John! Yoh kin. I knows mon'sous well dat yoh kin! He gwine ter do jes' what yoh tell 'im ter. I knows dat he is, Mis' Kate!"

Mr. Davenport was in his study. Katherine

had explained the case to him fully, and Sallie's black face peered in behind him, with anxious eyes, watching and listening to her mistress.

"Katherine, I cannot! I cannot pay money for a human being. I have yielded, step by step, to what I felt was wrong long ago, until now I am caught in the tangled threads of this awful system—but I cannot! I *cannot* pay money for a human soul!"

Suddenly Sallie fell at his feet, and, swaying to and fro, swung her sturdy frame like a reed in the wind.

"Oh, Mos' Grif, fo' God's sake, buy John! Ain't yo' got no mussy, Mos' Grif? Don' let dat Mos' Bradley sen' John 'way off dar! I gwine ter die right heah, if yo' don' hep me, Mos' Grif! Ain't I been a good girl? Ain't I nus de chillun good, an' did'n I pull Mos' Beverly outen de crick when he fall in an' wus mose drownded? Oh, fo' Christ's sake, Mos' Grif, buy my John! He gwine ter wuk fo' yoh all his life long, an' he gwine ter be good!"

She swayed and wept and moaned. She held her baby to her breast and cried out for John, and then she held it out toward Griffith and stared through streaming eyes at his face to see if he had relented. And still Griffith was silent. His teeth were set tight together, and his nails cut his palms, but he said not a word.

"Mos' Grif, Mos' Grif! what did God A'mighty gib yoh all dis lan' an' houses an' money fo'? What He gib yoh my Mis' Kath'rine fo'? 'Cause He know yoh gwine ter be good an' kine, an'—an' dat yoh gwine ter be good ter *us!* Mos' Grif, de good Lawd ain't fo'got we alls des kase we black!"

She rolled the baby on the floor beside her and grasped both of her master's clenched hands, and struggled to open them as she talked. She seemed to think if they would but relax that he would yield.

"Mos' Grif, we bofe gwine ter wuk fo' yoh, an' pray fo' yoh, and dat baby, dar, gwine ter wuk an' pray fo' yoh all ouh lifes long—all de days ob ouh lifes, des fo' dat little, teenchy six hund'ud dollahs, what Mos' Bradley got ter hab fo' John! All ouh lifes long! All ouh lifes long, we gwine ter wuk and pray fo' yoh, des fo' dat little, teenchy six hund'ud dollahs!!"

Mrs. Davenport put her hand on her husband's shoulder. Her eyes were wet and her lips trembled.

"Griffith, what harm can it do? And see how *much* good! Griffith, we will *all* love you better if you will. I can't bear to see Sallie the way she has been these last two months—ever since it was decided to sell John to that man when he comes. It is heart-breaking. You know, darling, she played with me ever since we were babies, and she has been *so* good to my children—*our* children, Griffith!" She lowered her voice to a mere whisper: "Can God want you to be so cruel as this, Griffith?"

Mr. Davenport had never dreamed that anything he might feel it his duty to do would seem to his wife like cruelty. It hurt him sorely. He looked up at her with a drawn face.

"Katherine," he said, "let us give Sallie her freedom, and let her go with John."

"No, no, no, no! I ain't gwine ter go wid dat man! I ain't gwine ter be no free wife nigger, 'pendin' on him! I ain't gwine ter leabe Mis' Kath'rine, nedder!" She arose in her fear, which was turning to wrath. "Mis' Kate, yoh ain't gwine ter let him gib me away, is yoh? I don' belong to nobody ter gib away, but des ter my Mis' Kate, an' she ain't gwine ter gib me 'way arter I done nus her chillun an' save de life of Mos' Beverly! Dat ain't de kine o' lady my Mis' Kate is! O Mis' Kate, Mis' Kate! I done wisht yoh'd a-gone and married dat Mos' Tom Harrison dat time wat 'e ax you! *He* don't lub money dat much dat he can't spahr a little six hund'ud dollahs ter sabe me an' John an'—an'—an' dis heah baby!"

She caught up the baby from the floor again and held it toward her master.

"Dar! take hit an' kill hit fus' as well as las'! kase *I* gwine ter die, an' hit gwine ter be my Mos' Grif dat kill bofe of us. God gwine ter know 'bout dat! John gwine ter tell 'im! Jesus gwine ter know dat six little hund'ud dollahs is wuf more ter my Mos' Grif dan me an' yoh an' John," she moaned, holding the baby up in front of her. "All free, bofe ob us, ain't wuf dat little much t' ouh Mos' Grif! All free, bofe ob us! A little, teenchy, ugly six hund'ud dollahs! He radder hab hit in de bank er in de desk er in he pocket—dat little six hund'ud dollahs what's mo' bigger dan *all* ob us—an' mo' bigger dan Mis' Kate's lub!" She fell to sobbing again. "Des dat little much! Des dat little much!" she moaned. "All ob us got ter die fer des dat little much! An' Mos' Grif, he don' care. He lub dat little much money mo' dan wat he do *all* ob us, countin' in Mis' Kate's lub wid de res'!"

His wife had gone to her chair and was holding a handkerchief to her face. He could see her lips and chin tremble.

"I will buy John, Sallie, if——"

Sallie grasped the two hands again. They were relaxed and cold.

"I knowed hit! I knowed hit! O good, kind Jesus! O Lord, Saviour! dey ain't no *if!* Dey ain't no if! My Mos' Grif gwine ter do hit. Dey ain't no if lef' in dem han's! My Mos' Grif gwine ter buy John!" and she fell on her knees again and sobbed for joy. She caught the little black baby up from the floor where it lay, laughing and kicking its toes in the air, and crushed it so close to her breast that it cried out and then set up a wail. Sallie stopped weaving her body to and fro, and tried to smile through her tears.

"Des listen ter dat fool baby! Hits cryin' fo' des a little hu't like dat, an' I only des choke hit wif my arms! Mos' Grif done choke my hawt out wid grief, an' now he done strangle me wid joy, befo' I got ter cry, chile! Yoah po' mammy's hawt done bus' wide open wid joy now. Dat's what make I can't talk no sense, Mos' Grif. I des wants ter yell. But Mis' Katherine, she know. I des kin see dat she do. *She* know dat I feel des like I gwine ter bus' plum' down ter my chist. She know!"

She laid the baby down again and suddenly held up both arms toward her master. Her voice was a wail.

"Tell me dat dey ain't no *if* lef' in your hawt, Mos' Grif! I knows dat dey ain't, but I got ter heah yo' *say* dat dey ain't, an' den I kin go!"

"I will buy John, Sallie. There is no if," he said; and Katherine threw her arms around his neck and looked at him through tears of joy.

That night the Rev. Griffith Davenport prayed long and earnestly that he might be forgiven for this final weakness. He felt that his moral fiber was weakening. He had broken the vow taken so long ago. He felt that the bonds were tightening about him, and that it would be harder than ever to cleanse his soul from what he had grown to feel was an awful wrong—this ownership, and now this money purchase, of a human soul.

"I have gone the whole length," he sighed to himself. "I have at last, with my eyes open, with my conscience against me, done this wrong! I have paid money for a human being. I know it is a wrong—I know—I know, and yet I have done it! God help me! God forgive me! I cannot see my way! I cannot see my way!"

In the distance, as he arose from his knees, there floated in through the open window the refrain from Sallie's song, as she moved about the quarters:—

> An' deys no mo' trouble, an' deys no mo' pain,
> An' deys no mo' trouble fo' me, fo' me!
> An' deys no mo' sorrer, an' no mo' pain—
> Oh, deys no mo' trouble fo' me, f-o-h-h m-e-e-e!
>
> I libs on de banks ob de golden shoah,
> Oh, I libs in de promise' lan'!
> An' I sez to de Lawd, when He opens the doah,
> Dat deys no mo' trouble fo' me!

> De Lawd He says, when he took my han',
> "Enter into de gates ob res'!"
> An' He gib me a harp, an' I jines de ban',
> Fo' deys no mo' sorrer fer me!

Lippy Jane was dancing, on the back porch, to the rhythm of the distant song, and two of the black boys stopped in their race with Beverly, over the lawn, to take up the chorus—"Oh, deys no mo' trouble fo' me, f-o-h m-e!"

But, in spite of his prayer for "light and leading," as he would have called it, Mr. Davenport felt that his moral fiber was, indeed, weakening, and yet he could not see his way out of the dilemma. He had definitely decided so long ago now that he could not remember when he had thought otherwise, that for one in his position, at least, even the mere ownership of slaves could not be right. He recalled that it had come to him at first in the form of purchase and sale, and it had seemed to him that under no conditions could he be forced into that form of the complication; but a little later on he decided that the mere ownership involved moral turpitude for one of his denomination, at least, if he was in deed and in truth following the leaderhip of the Christ.

When first he had agreed to take part of his father's slaves, therefore, he had made himself feel that it was right that he should assume a part of the old Major's burdens as his son and trustee, only, and that there was to be no transfer of property. That this service was his father's due and that he should give it freely seemed plain to him. Katherine's slaves he had always thought of as hers alone—not at all as his; but ever since the old Major had died and the will had settled beyond a quibble that the Rev. Griffith Davenport was himself, in deed and in truth "Mos' Grif" to all these dependent creatures, it had borne more and more heavily upon his conscience. He had tried to think and plan some way out of it and had failed, and now he had been forced to face the final issue— the one phase which he had felt could never touch him,—the purchase for money of a black man, and he had yielded at the first test! His heart had outweighed his head and his conscience combined, and the line he had fixed so long ago as the one boundary of this evil which *he* could never pass, and which, thank God, no one else could thrust upon him, was obliterated, and he stood on the far side condemned by his whole nature! In this iniquity from which he had felt his hands should forever be free, they were steeped! He felt wounded and sore and that a distinct step downward had been taken, and yet he asked himself over and over again what he could have done in the matter that would not have been far worse. He slept little. The next day when he went to Mr. Bradley to buy John his whole frame trembled and he felt sick and weak.

His neighbor noticed that he was pale, and remarked upon it, and then turned the subject to the matter in hand which Sallie had duly reported an hour after she had won and her master had lost the great moral contest. For it cannot be denied that, all things considered, Sallie had won a distinct victory for the future moral life of herself and for John and the baby. So complicated are our relations to each other and to what we are pleased to call right and wrong in this heterogeneous world, that in doing this Sallie had forced her master into a position which seemed to him to cancel his right to feel himself a man of honor and a credit to the religion in which he believed he had, so far, found all his loftiest ideals. He could plainly see, now, that this phase of the terrible problem would be sure to arise and confront him again and again as time went on, and his heart ached when he felt that he had lost his grasp upon the anchor of his principles and that the boundary lines of his ethical integrity were again becoming sadly confused in a mind he had grown to feel had long ago clearly settled and defined them.

"You look as pale as a ghost. Better try a little of Maria's blackberry cordial? No? Do you good, I'm sure, if you would," said Mr. Bradley. "You're taking this thing altogether too much to heart, sir. What possible difference can it make to John whether you pay for him or whether he had come to you as the others did? If you will allow me to say so, I think it is a ridiculous distinction. Somebody paid for the ones you've got. If you'll allow an old neighbor to make a suggestion, I think you read those Yankee papers altogether too much and too seriously. It perverts your judgment. It's a good sight easier for those fellows up there to settle this question than it is for us to do it. They simply don't know what they are talking about, and we do. With them it's all theory. Here it's a cold fact. What in the name of common sense would they have? Suppose we didn't own and provide for and direct all these niggers, what on earth would become of 'em? Where would they get enough to eat? You know as well as I do there is nothing on this earth as helpless and as much to be pitied as a free nigger. They don't know how to take care of themselves, and nobody is going to hire one. What in thunder do people want us to do? Brain 'em?"

"Oh, I know, I know," said Mr. Davenport, helplessly, looking far off into the beautiful valley, with its hazy atmosphere and its rich fields of grain. "I've thought about it a thousand times, and a thousand times it has baffled me. I'm not judging, now, for you, Mr. Bradley, not in the least. I feel myself too thoroughly caught in the meshes of our social fabric to presume to unravel it for other people. But—but in *my* position—for myself—it seems a monstrously wrong thing for me to count out this money and pay it over for John, just as if he were a horse. It makes me feel sick—as I fancy a criminal must feel after his first crime."

Mr. Bradley laughed.

"You don't look it, Davenport! Criminal! Ha, ha, ha, ha! that's rich!"

Griffith moved uneasily and did not join the laugh which still convulsed his neighbor.

"For *me* it is wrong—distinctly, absolutely wrong. It is a terrible thing for me to say—and still do it—I, a preacher of God! For you, I cannot judge. 'Judge not, that ye be not judged,' is what I always think in this matter. But for me, for *me* it is not right—and yet what can I do?"

Mr. Bradley laughed again, partly in amusement and partly in derision, at what he looked upon as the preacher's unworldly view, and what he spoke of with vexation to others as "Davenport's damned foolishness," which had, of late, grown to be a matter of real unrest to the neighborhood, in which it was felt that the influence of such opinions could not fail to be dangerous to social order and stability. It was as if you or I were to spring the question of free land or free money in a convention of landlords and bankers. Or, if you please, like the arguments for anarchy or no government addressed to the " Fourth ward," or the members of Congress. It was, in short, subversive of the established order of things, and neither you, nor I, nor they, accept quite gracefully such propositions, if in their application to ourselves, they would be a sore and bitter loss—if it would render less secure and lofty our seat on the social or political throne. We revolt and we blame the disturber of the old established order of things—the order, which having been good enough for our fathers is surely good enough for you and for me. In short, was not the way in religion and in social order of our fathers far the better way ? Is not the better way always that of the man who owns and rides in the carriage ? If you will ask him—or if you are he—you will learn or see that there is not the least doubt of the fact. If you should happen to ask the man who walks, you may hear another story—if the man who walks happens to be a philosopher ; but as all pedestrians are not philosophers and since acquiescence is an easy price to pay for peace, it may happen that the man in the carriage will be corroborated by the wayfarer whom his wheels have run down.

And so, my friend, in the year 1852, had you been sitting counting out the six hundred dollars which must change hands to enable John to play with the little black baby on his knee, after his day's work was done, and to keep Sallie from the pitiful fate she dreaded, it is to be questioned if you would not have agreed with Mr. Bradley in his covert opinion that " Davenport's squeamishness was all damned nonsense," and that he might far better stop reading those Yankee newspapers. But be that as it may, the deed was done. The transfer was made, and the Rev. Griffith Davenport rode home with a sad heart and troubled conscience. He did not sing nor even hum his favorite hymns as he rode. His usually radiant face was a study in perplexity. When he passed the cross-roads he did not whistle to the robin who always answered him.

Selim's successor and namesake slackened his gait and wondered. Then he jogged on, and when he stopped at the home " stile " and

Griffith still sat on his back, apparently oblivious of the fact that the journey was at an end. Selim whinnied twice before the responsive pat fell upon his glossy neck.

Jerry ran out. "Dinnah's raidy, Mos' Grif. Mis' Kath'rine she been a waitin' foh yoh."

The rider roused himself and dismounted, more like an old man than like his cheery, jovial, alert self.

"Is that so? Is it dinner-time already?" he asked absently. "Feed him, but don't put him up. I may want him again after dinner."

"You ain't sick, is you, Mos' Grif?"

"No, no, boy, I'm not sick," he said, and then recognizing the look of anxiety on the faithful fellow's face: "What made you ask that?"

"Yoh look so monst'ous lemoncholly, Mos' Grif. Hit ain't seem like yo'se'f. I des fought dey mus' be somp'in de mattah wid yo' insides."

Mr. Davenport laughed and snapped the riding whip at the boy. Jerry dodged the stroke, but rubbed the place where it was supposed to fall.

"Lemoncholly, am I? I'll lemoncholly you, you rascal, if you don't just knock off and go fishing this afternoon. I shan't need you with me."

He was half way to the house when he called back: "Bring me a nice mess of trout, boy, and you'll see my insides, as you call 'em, will be all right. It's trout I need. Now mind!"

And Jerry was comforted.

CHAPTER VII.

WHAT WOULD YOU HAVE DONE?

It was a year later before the Rev. Griffith Davenport found himself in a position to carry out, even in part, a long-cherished plan of his. For some time past, he had been strengthening himself in the belief that in the long run he would have to flee from the problem that so perplexed him. That he would have to make one supreme effort which should, thereafter, shield him against himself and against temptation. This determination had cost him the severest struggle of his life, and it had resulted in the rupture of several lifelong friendships and in strained relations with his own and his wife's near kinsmen. It had divided his church and made ill-feeling among his brother clergymen, for it had become pretty generally known and talked about, that the Rev. Griffith Davenport had definitely determined to leave his old home and take his sons to be educated "where the trend of thought is toward freedom" as he had expressed it, and as his neighbors were fond of quoting derisively. He had finally secured a position in connection with a small college somewhere in Indiana, together with an appointment as "presiding elder" in the district in which the college was located. He had arranged for the sale of his property, and he was about to leave.

To those whose traditions of ancestry all center about one locality, it costs a fearful struggle to tear up root and branch and strike out into unknown fields among people of a different type and class; with dissimilar ideas and standards of action and belief. To such it is almost like the threat or presence of death in the household. But to voluntarily disrupt and leave behind all of that which has given color and tone and substance to one's daily life, and at its meridian, to begin anew the weaving of another fabric from unaccustomed threads on a strange and unknown loom, to readjust one's self to a different civilization—all this requires a heroism, a fidelity to conscience and, withal, a confidence in one's own judgment and beliefs that surpass the normal limit. But, if in addition to all this, the contemplated change is to be made in pursuance of a moral conviction and will surely result in financial loss and material discomfort, it would not be the part of wisdom to ask nor to expect it of those who are less than heroic. In order to compass his plans Mr. Davenport knew that it would be necessary to dispose of his slaves. But how?

He hoped to take with him to his new home —although they would be freed by the very act—several of the older ones and Jerry and his little family. He knew that these would, by their faithful services, be a comfort and support to his wife and of infinite use and advantage to the children, whose love and confidence they had. To take all into his employ in the new home would, of course, be impossible. He would no longer have the estate of an esquire. At first, at least, he must live in a small town. There would be no land to till and no income to so support them. The house would no longer be the roomy mansion of a planter. His income would be too meager to warrant the keeping of even so many servants as they were planning to take—and there would be little work for them to do. The others must be disposed of in some other way. But how? They are yours, my friend, for the moment. How will you dispose of them? What would you have done?

"Free them and leave them in the state of their birth and of their love where their friends and kinsmen are?" But you cannot! It is against the law! If you free them you must take them away. Sell them? Of course not! give them to your wife's and your own people? Would that settle or only perpetuate and shift the question for which you are suffering and sacrificing so much? And it would discriminate between those you take and thus make free and those you leave and farther fix in bondage, and the Rev. Griffith Davenport had set out to meet and perform, and not merely to shift and evade, what he had grown to look upon as his duty to himself and to them. It was this which had burdened and weighed upon him all these last months, until at last he had determined to meet it in the only way that seemed to settle it once and for all. He would go. He would free all of them and take them with him into the state of his adoption. He would then give hired employment to those he needed in his household and the others would have to shift for themselves. This he prepared to do. Some of them would not want to go into a homeless and strange new land. This he also knew. Pete was, as the negroes phrased it, "settin' up to" Col. Phelps' Tilly. Pete would, therefore, resist, and wish to remain in Virginia. Old Milt and his wife had seven children who were the property of other people in the neighborhood, and their grandchildren were almost countless. It would go hard with Milt and Phillis to leave all these. It would go even harder with them to be free—and homeless. Both were old. Neither could hope to be self-supporting. My friend, have you decided what to do with Milt and Phillis? Add Judy and Mammy and five other old ones to your list when you have solved the problem.

Mr. Bradley had spoken to Griffith of all these things—of the hardships to both black and white—and of the possible outcome.

Over and over during the year, when they had talked of the proposed new move, he had urged these points.

"It seems to me, Mr. Davenport, that you are going to tackle a pretty rough job. You say you will take all of them as far as Washington, anyhow. Now you ought to know that there are no end of free niggers in Washington, already, with no way to support themselves. Look at Milt and Phillis and Judy and Dan, and those other old ones in the two end cabins! They've all served you and your father before you faithfully all of their lives, and now you are proposing to turn them out to die—simply to starve to death. That's the upshot of your foolishness. You know they won't steal, and they can't work enough to support themselves. All the old ones are in the same fix, and the young ones will simply be put on the chain-gang for petty thefts of food before you get fairly settled out west. Lord, Lord, man, you don't know what you are doing! I wish the old Major was here to put a stop to it. You're laying up suffering for yourself, you're laying up sorrow and crime for them, you are robbing your children of their birthright, and of what their grandfathers have done for them, you are making trouble among other people's niggers here who hear of it, and think it would be a fine thing to be a free nigger in Washington or Indiana—and what good is it all going to do? Just answer me that? It would take a microscope to see any good that *can* come out of it. It's easy enough to see the harm. Look at 'Squire Nelson's Jack! He undertook to run off last week, and Nelson had him whipped within an inch of his life. Yes, bad policy, and cruel, of course, but that's the kind of a man Nelson is. Now your move is going to stir up that sort of thing all around here. It does it every time. You know that. What in thunder has got into the heads of some of you fellows, I can't see. It started in about the time you Methodists began riding around here. Sometimes I think they were sent down here just for that purpose, and that the preaching was only a blind."

Mr. Davenport laughed. "Ha, ha, ha, ha! Bradley, you are a hopeless case! If I didn't know you so well, I'd feel like losing my temper; but——"

"Oh, I don't mean you, of course. I know *you* got to believing in the new religion and got led on. I mean those fellows who came down here and started it all when you were a good, sensible boy. And how do they get their foolishness, anyhow? Your Bible teaches the right of slavery plain enough, in all conscience, and even if it didn't, slavery is here and we can't help ourselves; and what's more we can't help the niggers by turning some of 'em loose to starve, and letting them make trouble for both the masters and the slaves that are left behind. I just tell you, Mr. Davenport, it is a big mistake and you are going to find it out before you are done with it."

Griffith had grown so used to these talks and to those of a less kindly tone that he had stopped arguing the matter at all, and, indeed, there seemed little he could say beyond the fact, that it was a matter of conscience with him. His wife's father had berated him soundly, and her sisters plainly stated that, in their opinion, "poor Brother Grif was insane." They pitied their sister Katherine from the bottom of their hearts, and thanked God devoutly that their respective husbands were not similarly afflicted. And, as may be readily understood, it was all a sore trial for Katherine.

At last, when the manumission papers came, Katherine sent LeRoy, her second son, to tell the negroes to come to the "big house."

Roy ran, laughing and calling, to the negro quarters. "Oh, John, Pete, Sallie, Uncle Milt everybody! Father says for *all* of you—every single one—to come to the big house right after supper! Every single one! He's got something for you. Something he is going to make you a present of! I can't tell you what—only every one will have it—and you must come right away after supper!"

"G'way fum heah, chile! What he gwine t' gib *me?* New yaller dress?" inquired Lippy Jane, whereupon there arose a great outcry from the rest, mingled with laughter and gibes.

"I know wat he gwine t' gib Lippy Jane! He gwine t' gib 'er a swing t' hang onter dat lip, yah! yah! yah!" remarked Pete, and dodged the blow that his victim leveled at him.

"New dress! Lawsy, chile, I reckon he be

mo' likely ter gib you a lickin' along 'er dat platter you done bus' widout tellin' Mis' Kate!" put in Sallie, whose secure place in the affections of the mistress rendered her a severe critic of manners and morals in the "quarters."

"Come heah, Mos' Roy, honey, an' tell ole Unc' Milt wat 'e gwine t' git. Wat dat is wat Mos' Grif gwine t' gib me? Some mo' 'er dat dar town terbacker? Laws a massy, honey, dat dar las' plug what he fotch me nebber las' no time er tal."

But Roy was tickling the ear of old Phillis with a feather he had picked up from the grass, and the old woman was nodding and slapping at the side of her head and humoring the boy in the delusion that she thought her tormentor was a fly. Roy's delight was unbounded.

"G'way fum heah, fly! Shoo! G'way fum heah! I lay dat I mash you flat 'fo' a nudder minnit! Sho—o—o!"

Roy and the twins were convulsed with suppressed mirth, and Aunt Phillis slapped the side of her head with a resounding whack which was not only a menace to the life and limb of the aforenamed insect, but also, bid fair to demolish her ear as well. One of the twins undertook to supplement the proceeding on the other ear with a blade of "fox tail," but found himself sprawling in front of the cabin door. "You triflin' little nigger! Don' you try none 'er yoah foolin' wid me! I lay I break yoah fool neck! I lay I do," exclaimed the old woman in wrath. Then in a sportively insistent tone, as she banged at the other side of her head, "Fore de good Lawd on high! twixt dat imperent little nigger an' dis heah fly, I lay I'm plum wore out. Sho-o-o, fly!"

Suddenly she swung her fat body about on the puncheon stool and gave a tremendous snort and snapped her teeth at the young master. "Lawsey me, honey, was dat yoh all dis long cum short? Was dat yo' teasin' yoah po' ole Aunt Phillis wid dat fedder? I lay I gwine ter ketch yo' yit, an' swaller yo' down whole! I lay I is!"

The threat to swallow him down whole always gave Roy the keenest delight. He ran for the big house, laughing and waving the feather at Phillis.

Great was the speculation in the quarters as to what Mos' Grif had for every one.

"Hit's des' lack Chris'mus!"

"I des wisht I knowed wat I gwine t' git."

"Lawsey me, but I wisht hit was arter supper now!"

In the twilight they came swaying up through the grass—a long irregular line of them. Jerry had his banjo. Mammy, Sallie's old mother, carried in her arms the white baby. Little Margaret was her sole care and charge and no more devoted lovers existed.

"Et me wide piggy back, mammy," plead the child.

"Heah, Jerry, put dis heah chile on my back! Be mons'ous keerful dar now! Don' yoh let dat chile fall! Dar yoh is, honey! Dar yoh is! Hol' tight, now! Hug yoah ole mammy tight! D-a-t-s de way.

"'Go down, Moses, away down in Egypt's lan',
Go tell ole Pharoah, t' let my people go.'"

Mammy began to trot and hum the tune for the child. The swaying rhythm caught like a sudden fire in a field of ripened grain. Every voice, old and young, fell into harmony, and Jerry's banjo beat its tuneful way like the ripple of a stream through it all.

Mrs. Davenport stood by the window watching them as they came nearer and nearer. Her face was sad and troubled. She looked up into the clear twilight and saw one star peer out. She did not know why, but in some mysterious way it seemed to comfort her. She smiled through dim eyes at the child on mammy's back. Her husband still sat by the table sorting over some legal-looking papers.

"Are those the manumission papers, father?" asked Beverly, taking one up and turning it curiously.

"Yes."

Beverly glanced at his father. It seemed to him that the lines in his face were very sad. The merry twinkle that always hid in the corners of eyes and mouth were obliterated. There was a settled look of anxiety. He seemed older. Beverly was silent. He more nearly understood what his father was doing than did even Katherine. Presently he said: "Hear them sing!"

Mr. Davenport was staring straight before him into space. He turned to listen.

"Happy, careless, thoughtless, unfortunate creatures," he said softly, "and as free as you or I, this minute—as free as you or I—if only they knew it;" then suddenly—"No, not that, either. They can never be *that* so long as they may not stay here free, even if they want to. I suppose I am breaking the law to tell them what I shall to-night, but I *can't* take them away from their old home and friends and not tell them it is for good and all—that they may not come back. For good and all—for good and all," he repeated, abstractedly. After a long pause he said, "Law or no law, I cannot do that. I must tell them they are free before they go—and that they must say good-bye, never to come back."

"Seems pretty hard, doesn't it, father? But then—but—don't you think God was pretty hard on them when He—when He made them black? Jerry is a gentleman, if—if he was not black."

"Griffith," asked Katherine from the window, "how do you suppose they will take it? I'm afraid——"

"Take it! take it! Why, little woman, how would you or I take freedom if it were given to us?" The thought cheered him and he crossed the room and tapped her cheek with the papers. His face beamed. "I'm prepared to see the wildest outbreak of joy." He chuckled, and some of the old lines of mirth came back to his face. "I'm glad Jerry brought his banjo. They will be in a humor for some of the rollicking songs afterward. I think they would do me good too. And you, you, little woman, you will need it too. You have been brave—you have been my tower of great strength in all this. If *you* had contested it, I'm afraid my strength would have given out, after all." He put his arm around her. "But God knows what we can stand, Katherine, and he tempers the trial to our strength. Thank God it is over—the worst of it," he said, and drew her to him.

Suddenly this silent, self-controlled woman threw both arms about his neck and sobbed aloud. "God help us to bear it, Griffith. Sometimes I think I cannot! It *is* hard! It is hard!"

He stroked her hair silently.

"Mos' Grif, does yoh want us to come in er t' stay on de big po'ch?" It was Jerry's voice. "Good-ebnin', Mis' Kath'rine! I hope yoh is monst'ous well dis ebenin'. Thanky, ma'am, yes'm, I'm middlin'."

Mrs. Davenport drew herself farther into the shadow, but she heard the little groan that escaped her husband. She understood. Her own voice was as steady as if no storm had passed.

"Open these large windows on to the porch, Jerry, and your Mos' Grif will talk to you from here. Just keep them all outside. I liked your songs. When Mos' Grif is done with you all, sing some more—sing that one he likes so well—the one about 'Fun in de Cabin.'"

"To be sho', Mis' Kath'rine, to be sho'. Dat I will. What dat Mos' Grif gwine ter gib us? Milt he 'low dat hit's terbacker, an' Lippy Jane she 'low dat hit's calicker, an' John he 'low dat——"

With the opening of the low windows a great wave of "howdys" arose and a cloud of black faces clustered close to the open spaces. The moon was rising behind them and the lamp on the table within gave but a feeble effort to rival the mellow light outside. The master was slow to begin, but, at last, when the greetings were over he said, with an effort to seem indifferent, "You all know that we are going away from here and that you are going, too; but——" He found the task harder than he had expected. His voice trembled and he was glad that Katherine put her hand on his arm. He shifted his position and began again. "You have all heard of freedom." He was looking at them, and the faces were so blandly, blankly vacant of that which he was groping for — they were so evidently expecting a gift of tobacco, or its like—that he omitted all he had thought of to say of their new freedom and what it could mean for them, and what it had meant for him to secure it for them, and at once held up the folded papers. "These are legal papers. They are all registered at a court-house. I have one for each one of you. These papers set you free! They are manumission papers, and you are all to be free! *free*——"

The silence was unbroken except for a slight shuffling of feet, but the dire disappointment was depicted on every face. That was too plain to be mistaken. Only papers! No tobacco! No calico! Nothing to eat! The silence grew uncomfortable. They were waiting for something for which they could give out the "thanky, Mos' Grif, thanky, sir. I's mighty much 'bleeged t' you. I is dat!" in their own hearty and happy way.

Griffith found himself trying to explain what these papers really were. He chanced to open Judy's first. He would make an object lesson of it. She had been his nurse, and was too old and rheumatic to work except as the spirit of occupation urged her to some trifling task. Griffith was reading the paper and explaining as he went. The negroes looked from the master to Judy and back again until he was done. She walked lamely to his side when he had finished and was holding her freedom papers toward her. She held out her hand for it. Then she tore it through twice and tossed it out of the window. Her eyes flashed and she held herself erect.

"What I want wid yoah ole mammermassent papers? What I want wid 'em, hey?" She folded her arms. "*Me* a free nigger! Me! Mos' Grif, yoh ain't nebber gwine ter lib t' be ole enough t' make no free nigger out ob ole Judy! What I fotch yoh up foh? Didn't I nus yoh fum de time yoh was a teenchy little baby, an' wasn't ole Mis' and yoah paw sas'fied wid me? What I done t' yoh now? What fo' is yoh gwine ter tun me loose dat a way? Mannermussent papers!" she exclaimed, in a tone of contemptuous wrath, "mannermussent papers! Yoh can't mannermusseut yoah ole Aunt Judy! Deys life lef' in her yit!"

It was done so suddenly. The reception of freedom was so utterly unexpected—so opposed to what he had fondly hoped—that Griffith stood amazed. Katherine motioned to mammy, who still stood with the white baby in her arms. "Give me the baby, mammy. I will——"

"Mis' Kate," said the old woman, turning, as she pushed her way through the room, "Mis' Kate, do Mos' Grif mean dat yo' alls is gwine ter *leabe* us? Do he mean dat *we alls* is got ter be free niggers, wid no fambly an' no big house an' no baby t' nus?"

She changed the child's position, and the little soft, white cheek lay contentedly against the black one.

"'Cause, if *dat's* wat Mos' Grif mean, dis heah chile ob yoahs an' ole mammy, deys gwine t' stay togedder. Dis heah mammy don't eben *tetch* no ole mannermussent papers! Tar hit up yo'se'f, Mis' Kate, kase dis heah nigger ain't eben gwine t' tetch hit. She's des gwine ter put dis baby ter bed lak she allus done. Goodnight, Mis' Kate! Good-night, Mos' Grif!"

She was half-way up the stairs, when she turned.

"Mis' Kate, sumpin' er a-nudder done gone wrong wid Mos' Grif's haid. Sho' as yoh bawn, honey, dat's a fack! I wisht yoh send fo' yoh paw. I does dat!" and she waddled up the stairs, with the sleeping child held close to her faithful heart.

The reception of the freedom papers by the others varied with temperament and age. Two or three of the younger ones reached in over the heads of those in front of them when their names were called, and, holding the papers in their hands, "cut a pigeon-wing" in the moonlight. One or two looked at theirs in stupid, silent wonder. Jerry and his wife gazed at the twins, and, in a half-dazed, half-shamefaced way, took theirs. Jerry took all four to Katherine. "Keep dem fo' me, please, ma'am, Mis' Kath'rine, kase I ain't got no good place fer ter hide 'em. Mebby dem dare chillun gwine ter want 'em one er dese here days."

Not one grasped the full meaning of it all. It was evident that one and all expected to live along as before—to follow the fortunes of the family.

"Thanky, Mos' Grif, much 'bleeged," said old Milt, as he took his, " but I'd a heap site a-rudder had some mo' ob dat town terbacker—I would dat, honey."

"Give it up for to-night, Griffith," said his wife, gently, as he still stood helplessly trying to explain again and again. "You look so white, and I am very tired. Give it up for tonight. It will be easier after they have talked it over together, perhaps—by daylight."

She pushed him gently into a chair and motioned to Jerry to take them all away. The faithful fellow remembered, when outside, that she had asked him to sing, but the merry song she had named had no echo in the hearts about him. All understood that they had failed to respond to something that the master had expected. The strings of his banjo rang out in a few minor chords, and as they moved toward the quarters an old forgotten melody floated back—

>O, de shadders am a'deep'nin' on de mountains,
> O, de shadders am a deep'nin' on de stream,
> An' I think I hear an echo f'um de valley,
> An echo ob de days ob which I dream!
>
>   Ole happy days!   Ole happy days!
> Befo' I knew dat sorrow could be bawn,
>   When I played wid mos'er's chillun in de medder,
> When my wuk was done a-hoein' ob de cawn!
>   Dose happy, happy days!   Dose happy, happy days!
> Dey'll come again no mo', no-o-o m-o-r-e, no more!
>
> Ole mos'er is a-sleepin' 'neath de willow!
>   An' de apple blossoms' fallin' on de lawn,
> Where he used to sit an' doze beneath its shadder,
>   In de days when I was hoein' ob de cawn!
>
>   Ole happy, etc.
>
> Dey'll come no mo' dis side de ribber Jordan,
>   O, dey'll come no mo' dis side de golden shoah!
> Foh de chillun's growed so big dat dey's forgot me,
>   Kase I'se ole an' cannot wuk foh dem no mo'!
>
>   Ole happy, etc.

CHAPTER VIII.

OUT OF BONDAGE.

"Look down. Say nothin'. Few words comprehends the whole."

The long, lank mountaineer stood leaning on his gun and looking listlessly at the collection of bundles, bags, children, dogs, guns, banjos, and other belongings of the Davenport negroes, as they waited about the wagons, now nearly ready to start for "Washington and the free States"—that Mecca of the colored race. It is true that Lengthy Patterson disapproved of the entire proceeding, notwithstanding his profound respect for, and blind admiration of, Parson Davenport, as he always called Griffith; but he had tramped many miles to witness the departure, which had been heralded far and wide. Lengthy's companion, known to his familiars as "Whis" Biggs, slowly stroked the voluminous hirsute adornment to which he was indebted for his name, "Whiskers" being the original of the abbreviation which was now his sole designation—Whis stroked his beard and abstractedly kicked a stray dog, which ran, howling, under the nearest wagon.

"Hit do appear t' me that the Pahrson air a leetle teched in the haid."

There was a long pause. The negroes looked, as they always did, at these mountaineers in contempt.

Lengthy dove into a capacious pocket and produced a large home-twisted hand of tobacco and passed it in silence to his companion, who gnawed off a considerable section and in silence returned it to the owner.

"Let's set," he remarked, and doubled himself down on a log. Lengthy took the seat beside him, and gathered his ever-present gun between his long legs and gazed into space. Mr. Biggs stroked his beard and remained plunged in deep thought. That is to say, he was evidently under the impression that he was thinking, albeit skeptics had been known to point to the dearth of results in his conversation, and to intimate that nature had designed in him not so much a thinker as an able-bodied rack upon which to suspend a luxuriant growth of beard. He was known far and wide as "Whis" Biggs; and, if there was within or without his anatomy anything more important, or half so much in evidence as was his tremendous achievement in facial adornment (if such an appendage may be called an adornment by those not belonging to a reverted type), no one had ever discovered the fact. What there was of him, of value, appeared to have run to hair. The rest of him was occupied in proudly displaying the fact. He stroked his beard and looked wise, or he stroked his beard and laughed, or he stroked his beard and assumed a solemn air, as occasion, in his judgment, appeared to require; but the occasion always required him to stroke his beard, no matter what else might happen to man or to beast.

But at last the wagons pulled out. Amidst shouts and "Whoas!" and "Gees!" and "G'langs!" Amidst tears and laughter and admonitions from those who went, and those who were left behind, the strange and unaccustomed procession took its course toward the setting sun. The family drove, in the old Davenport barouche, far enough behind to avoid the dust of the wagons. The long journey was begun for master and for freedmen. Each was launched on an unknown sea. Each was filled with apprehension and with hope. Old friends and relatives had gathered to witness the departure, some to blame, some to deprecate, and all to deplore the final leave-taking. Comments on the vanishing procession were varied and numerous. The two mountaineers listened in silence, the one stroking his beard, the other holding his gun. Some thought the preacher undoubtedly insane, some thought him merely a dangerous fanatic, some said he was only a plain, unvarnished fool; some insisted that since he had gone counter to public opinion and the law of the state, he was a criminal; while a semi-silent few sighed and wished for the courage and the ability to follow a like course. The first hours of the journey were uneventful. There was a gloom on all hearts, which insured silence. Each felt that he was looking for the last time upon the valley of their love. Jerry drove the family carriage. As they paused to lower the check-reins at the mill stream, Katherine bent suddenly forward and shaded her eyes with her hands. "Griffith! Griffith! there goes Pete back over the fields! I'm sure it is Pete. No other negro has that walk—that lope. See! He looked back! He is running! I know it is Pete!"

Mr. Davenport sprang from the carriage and shouted to the fleeing man. He placed his hands to the sides of his face and shouted again and again.

"Shell I run foh' 'im, Mos' Grif?" asked Jerry passing the lines to his mistress. "I lay I kin ketch 'im 'n I'll fetch' im back, too, fo' he gits to de cross-roads!"

He grasped the carriage whip and prepared to start. The shouts had served to redouble Pete's speed.

"He was your negro, Katherine, shall I let him go?" Griffith said in a tired voice.

"Yes, yes, oh, Griffith, let him stay in Virginia if he wants to. We can't have him with us—why, why not let him stay here?"

Griffith sighed. His wife knew quite well why; but she was nervous and overwrought and feared resistance should Pete be brought to bay—might he not fight for his freedom to remain where he might *not* be free!

The wagons had all stopped. One of the twins, with ashen face, came running back to report Pete's escape. "Mos' Grif, Oh, Lordy, Mos' Grif! Pete he's run off! Pete——"

It was plain to be seen that the negroes were restless and expectant. The tone and atmosphere of uncertainty among them, the tearful eyes of some, and the sullen scowl of others quickly decided Mr. Davenport. It was no time for indecision. Prompt action alone would prevent a panic and a stampede. Katherine spoke a few hasty words to him as he leaned on the carriage-door. He sprang in. "Go on!" he shouted. "Go on! We can't all stop now. We must cross the ferry to-night!" Then as a precaution he said to the twin: "Catch up and tell Judy that 'Squire Nelson will get Pete if he tries to stay here."

'Squire Nelson, the terrible! 'Squire Nelson! who had called before him a runaway boy and calmly shot him through the leg as an example to his fellows, and then sent him to the quarters to repent his rash act—and incidentally to act as a warning! 'Squire Nelson! Did the manumission papers give those who stayed behind to 'Squire Nelson? The negroes looked into each other's faces in silent fear, and drove rapidly on.

An hour later, as they were looking at the glorious sunset, and Griffith was struggling to be his old cheery self, Katherine said sadly: "We are as much exiled as they, Griffith. We could never come back." She choked up and then, steadying her voice, "If you think it is God's will we must submit; but—but everything makes it so hard—so cruelly hard. I am so afraid. I—no one ever—every one loved you before, and now—now—did you see the faces, Griffith, when we left? Did you see 'Squire Nelson's face?" She shuddered.

"Oh, is *that* all?" he exclaimed lightly. "Is that it, Katherine? Well, don't worry over that, dear. We won't be here to see it, and—of course he wouldn't like it. Of course it will make trouble among his negroes for awhile and I am sorry for that. I don't wonder he feels— I——"

"But, Griffith," she said nervously, "we are not out of the State yet, and—and, Griffith," she lowered her voice to make sure that Jerry would not hear, "can't the law do something dreadful to you for leaving Pete here, free? What can——"

"Jerry, I wish you'd drive up a little. Get to the ferry before it is too dark to cross, can't you?" said Griffith, and then, "Don't worry about that, Katherine, Pete won't dare show himself for a day or two, and besides——" He paused. The silence ran into minutes. Then he reached over and took her hand and with closed eyes he hummed as they rode, or broke off to point silently to some picturesque spot or to whistle to a robin. There was a nervous tension on them all.

"Mos' Grif, hit gwine ter be too late to cross dat ferry to-night. Ain't we better stop at dat big house over dar?"

Mr. Davenport opened his eyes. He had been humming—without time and with long pauses between the words—one of his favorite hymns. He looked out into the twilight, "That's Ferris's old mill and the Ferris house, isn't it, Katherine? Yes, Jerry, call to the boys to stop. We will have to stay over. It is too late to cross now. That ferry isn't very safe even in daylight."

The following morning, just before sunrise, there was a rap at the door, and a servant came to say that Mr. Davenport was wanted. Katherine was white with fear. She sprang from bed and went to the window. There, in front of the house, stood Lengthy Patterson, gun in hand, and beside him, sullen, crestfallen, and with one foot held in his hands, stood Pete. Griffith threw open the window, and Lengthy waited for no prelude. He nodded as if such calls were of daily occurrence, and then jerked his head toward Pete. "Saw him runnin'. Told him t' stop. He clim' out faster. Knowed you wanted him." He pointed to Pete's foot. It was bleeding. There was a bullet hole through the instep. "Few words comprehends the whole," added the mountaineer and relaxed his features into what he intended for a humorous expression. Griffith turned sick and faint. 'Squire Nelson's lesson had been well learned even by this mountaineer.

Pete was a dangerous negro to be without control, that was true. As a free negro left here without ties, it was only a question of time when he would commit some desperate deed, and yet what was to be done? Lengthy appeared to grasp the preacher's thought. He slowly seated himself on the front step and motioned Pete to sit on the grass.

"Don't fret. Take yer time. I'm a goin' t' the ferry. Few words comprehends th' whole," he remarked to Griffith, and examined the lock of his gun, with critical deliberation. When the wagons were ready to start Jerry whispered to his master that two of the other young negroes had run off during the night, and yet Mr. Davenport pushed on. It was not until late the next afternoon when the dome of the Capitol at Washington burst upon their sight that Griffith and Katherine breathed free. The splendid vision in the distance put new life and interest in the negroes. Their restlessness settled into a childlike and emotional merry-making, and snatches of song, and banter, and laughter told that danger of revolt or of stampede was over. Judy, alone, sulked in the wagons, and Mammy vented her discontent on the younger ones by word and blow, if they ventured too near her or her white charge. At last the Long Bridge alone stood between them and a liberty that could not be gainsaid—and another liberty for the master which had been so dearly and hazardously bought.

The Long Bridge was spanned and the strange party drove down Pennsylvania Avenue to the office of the attorney who had arranged for their reception. The Long Bridge was past and safety was theirs! Griffith glanced back and then turned to look. "Katherine," he said, smiling sadly, "we have crossed the dead line. We are all safe!" He sighed with the smile still on his lips.

"It is terrible not to feel safe! Terrible! Terrible!" she said in an undertone, "not to feel safe from pursuit, from behind, and from unknown and unaccustomed dangers near at hand—terrible!"

So accustomed had Griffith been to caring for and housing these negroes, who, now that they were in the midst of wonders of which they never had dreamed, clung to him with an abiding faith that whatever should betide he would be there to meet it for them—so accustomed had he been to caring for them that it had never occurred to Griffith not do so, even now when they were no longer his.

"Are the cabins ready?" he asked the attorney's clerk, and sent all but Mammy to the huts which had been provided on the outskirts.

"Go along with this gentleman, children," he said. "Mammy will stay with us, and after Jerry takes us to the hotel he will come and tell you what else to do. Good-bye! Good-bye! Keep together until Jerry comes."

All was uncertainty; but it was understood by all that several of the negroes were to go with the family and the rest to remain here. Griffith had decided to take to his new home Jerry and his wife, Ellen, and the twins; Mammy and Judy, and, if possible, Sally and John. It was here, and now, that he learned the inhospitality of the free states to the freed negroes.

"I intend to take several of them with me and——"

"Can't do it," broke in the attorney, "Indiana's a free state."

"Well, I can take 'em along and *hire* 'em, I reckon."

"Reckon you can't—not in Indiana."

"What!"

"I said you couldn't take 'em along and **hire** 'em."

"I'd like to know the reason for that. I——"

"Law. Law's against it."

Griffith drew his hand across his face as if he had lost his power to think.

"You can't take *any* of 'em to Indiana, I tell you," said the attorney insistently, and Griffith seemed dazed. Then he began again:

"Can't take them!" he exclaimed, in utter dismay.

"That's what I said twice — can't take them—none of them."

"But I shall pay them wages! Surely I can take my own choice of servants into my own household if they are free and I pay them wages! Surely——"

"Surely you *cannot*, I tell you," said the

attorney, and added dryly, "not unless you are particularly anxious to run up against the law pretty hard." He reached up and took down a leather-bound volume. He turned the leaves slowly, and Griffith and Katherine looked at each other in dismay. "There it is in black and white. Not a mere law, either—sometimes you can evade a law, if you are willing to risk it; but from the way you both feel about leaving those two free niggers in Virginia, I guess you won't be very good subjects for that sort of thing—thirteenth article of the constitution of the State itself." He drew a pencil mark along one side of the paragraph as Griffith read. "Oh! you'll find these free states have got mighty little use for niggers. Came here from one of 'em myself. Free or not free, they don't want 'em. You see," he said, slowly drawing a line down the other side of the page, "they prohibit you from giving employment to one! Don't propose to have free nigger competition with their white labor. Can't blame 'em." He shrugged his shoulders.

Griffith began to protest. "But I have read—I thought——"

"Of course you thought—and you've read a lot of spread-eagle stuff, I don't doubt. Talk is one of the cheapest commodities in this world; but when it comes to acts—" he chuckled cynically, "s'pose you had an idea that the border States were just holding out their arms to catch and shield and nurture and feed with a gold spoon every nigger you Southern men were fools enough to set free; but the cold fact is they won't even let you bring them over and pay 'em to work for you! That is one of the charming little differences between theory and practice. They've got the theory and you've had the practice of looking after the niggers! Your end is a damned sight more difficult than theirs, as you'll discover, if you haven't already. Excuse me, I forgot you were a preacher. You don't look much like one." Griffith smiled and bowed. Katherine had gone to the front window, where Mammy and the baby were enjoying the unaccustomed sights of the street. Griffith and the lawyer moved toward them.

"No, sir, your niggers have all got to stay right here in Washington and starve or steal.

You can't take 'em to Indiana, that's mighty certain. Why, when that Constitution was passed only a year or two ago, there wern't but 21,000 voters in the whole blessed State that didn't vote to punish a white man for even giving employment to a free nigger. Public sentiment as well as law is *all* against you. You can't take those niggers to Indiana—that's certain!"

"Dar now! Dar now! wat I done tole you?" exclaimed Mammy. "What I done tole Mos' Grif 'bout all dis foolishness? Mis' Kate, you ain't gwine ter 'low dat is you? Me an' Judy free niggers! *Town* free niggers wid no fambly!" The tone indicated that no lower depth of degradation and misfortune than this could be thrust upon any human being.

"I's gwine ter keep dis heah baby, den. Who gwine ter take cahr ob her widout me?" The child was patting the black face and pulling the black ear in a gleeful effort to call forth the usual snort and threat to "swaller her whole."

"Bless yoah hawt, honey, yoh ain't gwine t' hab no odder nus, is yo'? Nus! Nus!

White trash t' nus my baby! Yoh des gwine ter hab yoh ole mammy, dat's wat!"

The attorney took Mr. Davenport and Katherine to an inner office. It was two hours later when they came out. Both were pale and half dazed, but arrangements had been made, papers had been drawn, by which the nine oldest negroes were, in future, to appear at this office once every three months and draw the sum of twenty-four dollars each, so long as they might live. The younger ones must hereafter shift, as best they could, for themselves. The die was cast. The bridges were burned behind them. There was no return, and the negroes were indeed, " free, town niggers," henceforth.

" God forgive me if I have done wrong," said Griffith, as he left the office. " If I have done wrong in deserting these poor black children, for children they will always be, though pensioned as too old to work! Poor Mammy, Poor Judy! And Mart, and old Peyton!"

He shook his head and compressed his lips as he walked toward the door, with a stoop in his shoulders that was not there when he had entered. All the facts of this manumission were so wholly at variance with the established theories. Every thing had been so different from even what Griffith had expected to meet. As they reached the door the attorney took the proffered hand and laughed a little, satirically.

"Now I want you to tell me what good you expect all this to do? What was the use? What is gained? It's clear to a man without a spy-glass what's *lost* all around; but it's going to puzzle a prophet to show where the gain comes in, in a case like this. If you'll excuse the remark, sir, it looks like a piece of romantic tom-foolery, to a man up a tree. A kind of tom-foolery, that does harm all around—to black and to white, to bond and to free. Of course if *all* of 'em were free it would, no doubt, be better. I'm inclined to think that way, myself. But just tell me how many slave-owners —even if they wanted to do it—*could* do as you have? Simply impossible! Then, besides, where'd they go—the niggers? Pension the whole infernal lot? Gad! but it's the dream of a man who never will wake up to this world, as it is built. And what good *have* you done? Just stop long enough to tell me that;" he insisted, still holding Griffith's hand. He was smiling down at his client who stood on a lower step. There was in his face a tinge of contempt and of pity for the lack of worldly wisdom.

"I'm not pretending to judge for you nor for other men, Mr. Wapley, but for myself it was wrong to own them. That is all. That is simple, is it not?" The lawyer thought it was, indeed, very, very simple; but to a nature like Griffith's it was all the argument needed. His face was clouded, for the lawyer did not seem satisfied. Griffith could not guess why.

"My conscience troubled me. I am not advising other men to do as I have done. Sometimes I feel almost inclined to advise them *not* to follow my example if they can feel satisfied not to —the cost is very great—bitterly heavy has the cost been in a thousand ways that no one can ever know but the man who tries it—and this little woman, here." He took her hand and turned to help her into the carriage.

"Ah, Katherine, you have been very brave! The worst has fallen on you, after all—for no sense of imperative duty urged you on. For *my* sake you have yielded! Her bravery, sir, has been double, and it is almost more than I can bear to ask it—to accept it—of her! For my own sake! It has been selfish, in a sense, selfish in me."

Katherine smiled through dim eyes and pressed her lips hard together. She did not trust herself to speak. She bowed to the attorney and turned toward Mammy and the baby as they stood by the carriage door.

"I'm a-goin' wid yoh alls to de hotel, ain't I, Mis' Kath'rine? Dar now, honey, des put yoah foot dar an' in yoh goes! Jerry, can't yoh hol' dem hosses still! Whoa, dar! Whoa! Mos' Beverly, he radder set in front wid Jerry, an' I gwine ter set inside wid de baby, an' yo' alls."

The old woman bustled about and gave orders until they were, at last, at the door of the Metropolitan, where, until other matters were arranged, the family would remain.

Strange as it may seem, to save themselves from the final trial of a heartbreaking farewell, from protests, from the sight of weeping children and excited negroes, three days later

Mr. Davenport and his family left by an early train for the west before the negroes, aside from Jerry, knew that they were gone. And in the place of the spectacle of a runaway negro escaping from white owners, the early loungers beheld a runaway white family escaping from the galling bondage of ownership!

CHAPTER IX.

"One touch of nature."—*Shakespeare.*

As time wore on the family had, in some sort, at least, adjusted itself to the new order of things. The dialect of the strapping Irishwoman who presided over the kitchen of the small but comfortable new home, and the no less unaccustomed speech of the natives, themselves, were a never failing source of amusement to the children and, indeed, to Griffith himself. His old spirits seemed to return as he would repeat, with his hearty laugh, the village gossip, couched in the village forms of speech.

Each day as he opened his *Cincinnati Gazette* he would laugh out some bit of town news which he had overheard at the post-office or on his way home. The varying forms of penuriousness exhibited in the dealings between the farmers and the villagers impressed him as most amusing of all. The haggling over a few cents, or the payment of money between neighbors for fruit or milk or services of a nature which he had always looked upon as ordinary neighborly courtesy, filled him with mirth. One day, shortly after their arrival, Beverly had brought his mother a dozen peaches from a neighbor's yard. The boy had supposed when asked if his mother would not like them that they were intended as a present. He thanked the owner heartily and said that he was sure his mother would very greatly enjoy them.

"After he gave them to me," the boy said, indignantly, 'Six cents wuth, an' cheap at that!' says he, and held out his hand! Well, I could have fainted! Selling twelve peaches to a neighbor! Why, a mountaineer wouldn't do that! And then he had *asked* me to take them! I had ten cents in my pocket and I handed it to him and walked off. He yelled something to me about change, but I never looked back."

His father enjoyed the joke, as he called it, immensely. He chuckled over it again and again as he sat in the twilight.

One day late in that summer—the summer of

'57—the children were attracted by a great uproar and noise in the street. A group of school children, some street loafers, and a few mature but curious, grown citizens were gathered about an object in the middle of the street. Hoots and shouts of derision went up. A half-witted girl circled slowly about the outskirts of the crowd making aimless motions and passes with her hands toward the object of interest. Voices clashed with voices in an effort to gain coherent sound and sense. Was it a bear or a hand organ? The children ran to see. Beverly followed more slowly. Beverly seemed a young man now, so sedate and dignified was this oldest son.

"What is it?"

"Look out there! Look out there! It's going that way!"

"What? What you say? Who?"

"Who is Mosgrif? No man by that name don't live here."

"Nigger, nigger, pull a trigger, never grow an inch a bigger!"

"Get her some soap! Let's take her and give her a wash!"

"What? Who? Shut up your noise there, will you, Dave Benton. She's askin' fer somebody—some feller she knows. Who?"

There was a pause in the progress of the procession as it reached Mr. Davenport's side gate. Beverly was craning his neck to see over the heads of the crowd. His two brothers took a surer method. They dodged under arms and between legs and were making straight for the center of the crowd where they had heard an accustomed voice.

"What I axes yo' alls is, whah's my Mos' Grif! Dey done tole me down yander dat he lib down dis a-way. Whah's my Mos' Grif's house? I got ter fine my Mos' Grif!"

"Aunt Judy! Aunt Judy!" shrieked the two younger boys, in mad delight. "It's Aunt Judy! Oh, Beverly, come quick! She's hurt! She's been struck with a rock! Come quick—quick!"

LeRoy had reached the old woman, who began to tremble and cry as soon as she felt that friends were indeed near. She threw her arms about his neck and half-sobbed with joy. Then she tried to pick up the younger boy in her arms, as of old, but her strength gave way, and she fell on her knees beside her bundle and stick. A laughing shout went up. Dave Benton shied a small stone at her.

"How dare you! How dare you! you common loafers!" shrieked LeRoy, white with rage. He struck out with both fists at those who were nearest. "How dare you throw at Aunt Judy! How dare you, you low-down——!"

Words failed him, and he was choking with rage, but both fists were finding a mark on the visage of the prostrate Dave. His fists and the astonishment felt at the sight of white children caressing and calling the old black creature "aunty" had served to clear a space about them. Every one had fallen back. The half-witted girl alone remained with the center-group, making aimless passes, with ill-regulated hands, at Aunt Judy. So absorbing was this strange creature to the bewildered senses that not even the struggling boys on the ground at her feet served to divert her gaze from the old black face.

"His aunt's a nigger!"

"Kissed her, by gum!"

"They're the Virginia preacher's kids!"

"Never knew before that some of their kin was niggers!"

Dave Benton was now on top, and Howard was pulling at his leg in an effort to help his brother. Suddenly Roy swirled on top and grasped the helpless Dave by the throat.

"You let her alone, you dirty little — devil!" he ground out between his teeth, " or I'll *kill* you!"

His rage was so intense, his face was so set and livid, that it looked as if he might execute the threat before the astonished and half-amused bystanders realized the danger. Beverly sprang to the rescue. He had hustled Judy through the side gate and into the house with Howard.

"LeRoy! LeRoy! stop—stop! Get up! let go! Get up this instant!" he commanded, loosening the boy's grasp. "Look at that blood! Father will be so ashamed of you!"

He pushed the boy ahead of him and the door closed behind them, leaving a hooting mob outside and Dave Benton with a bleeding nose and a very sore head.

"Got a nigger fer a ant, by gosh!" exclaimed one, as they turned slowly away, leaving the weak-minded girl alone circling about the gate, making inarticulate noises and movements of indirection at the house and its curious and uncanny new occupant.

But LeRoy's blows and his taunts bore fruit in due season. A week later, Dave Benton's father, who had nursed his wrath, caused service to be made upon Mr. Davenport to show cause why he was not infringing the law and the State constitution by keeping in his service a free negro. Mr. Davenport explained to the court that he had not brought her into the State and was in no way responsible for her having come. Indeed, Judy would not or could not tell exactly how she had managed it herself. That she had been helped forward by some one seemed evident. But Griffith's plea would not suffice. She was here. He was avowedly the cause of her coming. She was a free negro. He was giving her employment. That was against the State constitution. Clearly, she must be sent away. Griffith consulted with a lawyer. The lawyer gravely stated, in open court, that the old negro was a guest, and not an employé, of the Davenport family. The judge smiled. There was no law, no constitutional provision, no statute to prevent a family from having negro guests in Indiana; provided they would give bond for the good behavior during life, and burial in case of death, of such guest!

"By gum! I reckon she *is* kin to 'em, shore 'nuff!" remarked Dave's father, *sotto voce*. "Wonder which one's sister she is—her'n or his'n?"

"Do' know, but it's one er t'other; fer all three o' the boys call her ant, 'n' the little gal, too. She rides on her back. Seen her out in the yard t'other day."

"'Fore I'd let one o' *mine* kiss a nigger 'n' ride on her back!"

"Well, *I* should smile!"

"Sh! What's that the jedge said?"

"Goin' t' take it under 'dvisement, perviden' Davenport agrees t' bind hisself—give bon'."

And so it came about, as I told you in the beginning, that this man, who was already a law-breaker in his native State, unblushingly became a law-evader in the State of his adoption;

for the papers were duly drawn up and finally signed and executed. Aunt Judy was officially and legally declared not to be employed by, but to be a visitor in, the family: "and, furthermore, it is declared and agreed, that, in case of her becoming indigent, or in case of her death while within the borders of the State, the aforenamed Rev. Griffith Davenport binds himself, his heirs and assigns, to support while living, or bury in case of the death of the aforenamed Judy Davenport (colored); and, furthermore, agrees that she shall in no manner whatsoever become a charge upon the State of Indiana. The expenses of this procedure to be paid, also, by the said Rev. Griffith Davenport."

"I reckon my conscience is getting a little tough, Katherine," said her husband, smiling, that night as he recited the matter to the family. "I signed that paper with precious little compunction—and yet it *was* evading the law, pure and simple—so far as the intent goes! Fancy Aunt Judy looking upon herself as a guest of the family! Ha! ha! ha! ha!" The idea so amused him that he laughed uproariously. Five minutes later there floated out on to the porch, where Judy sat with the children telling them wonderful tales of Washington, the notes of " Joy to the world! The Lord has come!"

" De *good* Lawd, bless my soul!" exclaimed the old woman, listening. " I ain't heerd nothin' so good as dat soun' ter me, sense yo' alls runned away! Dat sholy do soun' like ole times! Hit sholy do!"

Rosanna, the Irish cook, sniffed. She was hanging out of the kitchen window listening to aunt Judy's tales of adventure. " She do talk the quarest, schure, an' it's barely the rear av her remarks thet a Christian can understhand;" mumbled Rosanna to herself.

" Well, but how about the twins, Aunt Judy? You said you'd tell us all about the twins just as soon as supper was over. Now, hurry, or I'll have to go to bed," urged Howard.

The old woman shifted around in her chair to make sure the ears of Rosanna were not too near and lowered her voice to a stage whisper.

" Honey, dem dar twins is des so spilt dat dey is gettin' tainty!"

" Bad, you mean?" asked Roy.

" Dat's wat I said, an' dat's wat I sticks to.

Dey's so spilte dey's tainty. Bad! Why bad ain't no name fo' hit. Dey is mouldy. De onliest reason why dey ain't in the lock-up is kase dey ain't got ketched up wid yit. Dey gwine ter git dar, sho' as yoh bawn. Dey is dat!"

"I don't believe it. I don't believe the twins are so bad. You are just mad at 'em. They——" Roy was always a partisan.

"Look a heah, honey, yoh don't know what yoh's talkin' 'bout. Dem twins is plum spilte, I tell yoh. Jerry, he's a teamin' an' he can't watch 'em, an' dey maw she's a wuckin' fo' one er dem Congressers, an' dem twins is des plum run wile."

"Perhaps you expect too much of the morals of Washington," suggested Beverly, winking at Roy to give the old woman full sway.

"Mo'ls! mo'ls! Why, lawsy, honey, yoh don' know what yoh talkin' 'bout no mo' dan Mos' Roy do. Dey *ain't* no mo'ls in Washin'ton—white *ner* black. Mebby dem dar folks had some 'fo dey cum dar; but dey sholy did leave de whole lot back in de place whah dey cum fum! Dey sholy did dat. Mo'ls! In

Washin'ton? Dey ain't none dar!" She shook her finger at Beverly.

Roy saw his opportunity as she started for the door to shut off further questions. "Oh! go away, Aunt Judy, you don't know what morals are," he said, "that's all. In Washington they are government property and they keep 'em in tin cans. Of course you didn't *see* any."

"Dey dun los' de opener t' dat can, too," she remarked, hobbling up the steps. Many and blood-curdling had been her stories of life at the capital. In her opinion, the seat of government had no redeeming qualities. "Stay dar? Why, dis chile wouldn't stay dar fo' no 'mount o' money, ner fer *nobody*. She's got too much self-'spect fer *dat*, de good Lawd he do know. Stay dar? No, sah!"

"Well, the others are getting along all right, I'll bet you," piped up Howard, as her foot struck the top step. She turned.

"I ain't gwine ter tell yoh no mo' to-night. I'se gwine ter bed; but wat I knows is des dis: De way dey gets 'long, dey goes t' dat dar Mr. Lawyer an' gits dat money Mos' Grif done lef'. De fus' mont' dey sholy dus lib high; de nex' mont' dey sorter scrabbles erlong, an' de las' mont' dey sholy is hawd times. Dey ain't no use talking, dey sholy is dat! Now I'm des' gwine in 'n take a good big jorum of pepsissiway for my stummick, 'n git erlong ter my bed, fore de rusters 'gin ter crow fer mawnin'." And she disappeared in the darkness, shaking her head and reiterating the refrain, as to the badness of those twins.

The story of Aunt Judy's travels, in so far as she vouchsafed to tell them and not to resort to fiction or silence — her adventures by land and water, by wagon and rail, in search of "Mos' Grif," spread far and wide. The old woman could not set her foot outside of the door without a following of boys and girls, and, as a faithful historian, it would little avail me to omit, also, of men and of women, who hooted, stared at and otherwise indicated that she was less than human and more than curious. She was the pariah of the village, albeit LeRoy's fists had done their perfect work in that she was no more stoned. But she was content—so, at least, she asserted—and not even the longing for Jerry and Ellen and those badly-spoiled twins (of whom she never tired talking) served to convince her that there could be, on all this green earth, any home for her except, alone, the one that sheltered "Mos' Grif an' Mis' Kath'rine an' dat blessed baby," now grown too large to be a baby longer except alone to this loving old soul, to whom, forever, she was " my baby."

CHAPTER X.

"To thine own self be true." *Shakespeare.*

THERE had been a bright side for Griffith in all this change, too. New and warm friends had been made. He had watched with a feeling of joy the enervating influence of slave ownership drop from Beverly's young shoulders —and upon the other boys he felt that it had never cast its blight with a power that would outlast early youth. It filled him with pleasure to find his sons surrounded in the academy and college with the mental atmosphere and influence of freedom, only. He encouraged them to join the debating societies and Greek letter orders which admitted discussion of such topics. Beverly was now in his Sophomore year and was an ardent student of free-soil doctrines. He read and absorbed like a fresh young sponge the political literature of the time. He was always ready and eager to enter the debates of his class upon the ever pregnant and always recurring slavery extension and compromise bills. The young fellows had numerous hot arguments over the position of the different statesmen of the time, and Stephen A. Douglas furnished Beverly with many a hard hour's thinking. Mr. Davenport adhered to Douglas; but Beverly inclined to persistently oppose his point of view. When, at last, Douglas had taken the side of repeal in that famous measure—the Missouri Compromise Bill, which had been at once the hope and the despair of all the great northwest,—Beverly no longer hesitated. He and his father took different sides, finally and forever, in their political opinions. At commencement time, year after year, the governor of the State was made the feature of the college exercises, and he had several times been the guest of Mr. Davenport. This had served to draw to the house many politicians whose talks had given both stimulus and material to Beverly's already ardent political nature, which was so fast leading him outside the bounds reached by his father. The scope and class of his reading often troubled his mother sorely. One day she had gone to Griffith in dismay. It was so seldom that she felt obliged to criticise this eldest son of hers, upon whom she looked with a pride almost beyond words to express, that Griffith was astonished.

"I wish, Griffith, that you would tell Beverly not to read this book. It is the second time I have told him and he is determined. I burned the first copy and he has bought another. He says he will buy fifty if I burn them before he has read it all. He is that determined to read it. I hated to tell you, but——"

Griffith held out his hand for the obnoxious book. Then he exclaimed in surprise: "The 'Age of Reason'! Paine's book! Where did he happen to get that?" He looked over the title page.

"I see, I see! 'Rights of Man'—he quoted from that in his last essay at college. It was good, too—excellent. I've never read either one, but—oh, tut, tut, mother, why not let him read it? I wouldn't worry over it. Beverly is all right. He has got a better mind than you have—a far better one than I have—why not let him use it? Let him read anything he wants to. We can't judge for him. He'll be all right anyhow. You know that. He and I differ in politics now. He is going the radical road and I'm staying by the old line whigs; but— oh, tut, tut, Katherine! let's not hamper the boy's mind with our notions to the extent of forcing them on him. It won't do a bit of good if we try it either. That's not the kind of a mind Beverly has got—and suppose it was, what right have we to warp and limit its action?" He was turning over the leaves. "I've never read this myself." Then looking up suddenly: "Have you?"

"No, of course not! But my father forbade our boys reading it. He said it was a fearful book—infidel——" She broke off, but stammered something about Beverly's salvation. Griffith drew her down on his knee.

"Madam Kath'rine," he said, quizzically, "if I had followed my father's conscience instead of my own, I never would have"—he was going to say seen her, but he recognized in time that that might hurt her—"I never would have done a good many things that have seemed right to me—*the* only right things for my soul. So long as Beverly is open and frank and true to himself—and he has always been that—I mean to let him alone. I am sure that I found a good deal better way for myself than my father had marked out for me. Perhaps Beverly will. Suppose we trust him. He has been such a good son — such a frank fellow; don't let us make a pretender of him. Let him read what he does openly. You may be very sure if it looks wrong to him he won't *want* to be open with it. I don't want to hurt Beverly as my father, dear soul, hurt me—intending it for my own good, of course; but—but—can't you trust Beverly, Katherine? I can. And maybe, after all, people have not understood this book. Leave it here. I believe I'll read it myself."

Katherine was astonished, but the little talk rested and helped her. That night the book was on Beverly's table again and nothing was said of it. Beverly had joined his father's church when he was a little fellow, but since he entered college he had seemed to take slight interest in it. He was always present at family prayers, but said nothing about his religious views of late. A year ago he had been reprimanded, in company with others, by the local preacher for attending a social dance. That night he said to Roy: "The first time a dancing teacher comes to this town I am going to take lessons. Look at those Louisville boys in my class and in yours, too. They are twice as easy in their manners as any of the rest of us. It is their dancing that did it. They told me so."

"Mr. Brooks will turn you out of the church if you do," said Roy.

"Father wouldn't," replied Beverly, whistling—"and father is good enough for me."

But, since there had been no opportunity to fulfill the threat, the little matter of the social dance had blown over, and Beverly was still, nominally, a member of the Methodist Church.

The days passed. The political crash was upon the country. Men met only to talk of free-soil and slave extension, of union and disunion, of repeal, and even, in some quarters, of abolition. Young men's blood boiled. In Legislature and Congress feeling ran to blows. The air was thick and heavy with threats of— no one knew what. Old friendships were broken and new ones strained into real enmity. Brothers took different sides. Fathers and sons became bitter. Neighbor looked with suspicion upon neighbor. College fraternities lapsed into political clubs. It was now Beverly's last year. His favorite professor died. Griffith noticed that the boy was restless and abstracted. One day he came to his father.

"Father," he said, abruptly, "I don't feel as if I ought to waste any more time at college. There is a tremendous upheaval just ahead of us. Could you—would you just as soon I should?—I've got an offer with two of the other fellows, and I——"

Mr. Davenport recognized in the boy's unusual hesitancy of speech an unaccustomed quality of unrest and uncertainty. He looked over his gold-bowed glasses.

"Why, what is it, son? Out with it," he said, smiling.

"Well, it's like this: You remember Shapleigh, of the class last year? Well, you know his father owns that little free-soil paper out in Missouri that I get every once in a while. It's democratic, you know, but free-soil."

Griffith nodded. "Very good little paper, too. Don't fully agree with those last editorials—too fiery—but a very decent little sheet."

Beverly was evidently pleased.

"Well, the old gentleman is tired of the fight, and Shap wrote me that if Donaldson and I will each put in $1,500, his father will turn the paper over to the three of us. Shap knows how to run the business end of the concern. That's what he has done since he was graduated. Shap wants me for political editor, mostly. He's a red-hot free-soiler, and he knows I am. I sent him my last two speeches and he used 'em in the paper. He says they took like wild-fire; his constituents liked 'em first-class. You know, I've always thought I'd like to be a newspaper man. Think so more than ever now. Times are so hot, and there is such a lot to be said. They need new blood to the front, and——"

Griffith was laughing gently and looking quizzically, with lips pursed up, at this ambitious son of his; but the boy went on:

"The fact is, father, I've worried over it all this term. I hated to ask you if you could let me have the money. It is such a splendid chance—one of a lifetime, I think. I do wish you'd let me."

At last he had fallen into his boyish form of speech, and Griffith laughed aloud.

"*Let* you? *Let* you be an editor of a fiery free-soil paper out in Missouri, hey? The fellow that edits a paper out there just now can't be made out of very meek stuff, Bev. It won't be a nest of roses for any three young birds that try it, I reckon. D'yeh see that account in the *Gazette*, yesterday, of the mob out there near Kansas City?"

"Yes, I did; and that's the very thing that decided me to ask you to-day. Of course, you'd really own the stock. It would only be in my name till I could pay you for it, and——"

"Beverly," said his father, gravely, "if you've made up your mind fully to this thing, and are sure you know what you want and can do, I reckon you don't need to worry over the money for the stock. But are you *sure* you want to leave college before you finish? Isn't it a little premature?"

He did not hear his son's reply. It came

suddenly to his mind that this boy of his was almost exactly the age that he had been when he had tried to argue his own case with the old Major. It rushed into his thoughts how hard it had been to approach the topic nearest his heart, and how cruelly it had all ended. He realized, as he often did these days, how boyish and immature he must have seemed to his father, and yet how tragically old he had felt to himself. He wondered if Beverly felt that way now. He began to realize that the boy was still talking, arguing and planning, although he had not heard.

"Bev," he said, gently, using the abbreviation instinctively to make the boy feel the tenderness of his intent—"Bev, I don't intend to argue this thing with you at all."

Beverly had misunderstood his father's long silence and abstraction. The remark confirmed his misconception. He arose, disappointed, and started for the door. Griffith reached out, caught him by the sleeve, and pulled him into a chair beside his own.

"I want to tell you something, Bev. When I was about your age—maybe a little younger—

I made a request of my father that it had cost me a sore trial to make up my mind to ask. He—well, he didn't take it kindly, and—and—and I left home in a huff; not exactly a huff, either; but, to tell the truth, we succeeded in hurting each other sorely. And there wasn't the least need of it. It took us both a long time to get over the hurt of it. I sometimes doubt if we ever did get really all over it. I tell you, Beverly, boy, it was a sad, sad blunder all around. It darkened and dampened my spirits for many a day, and I don't doubt it did his."

Griffith was playing idly with a paper-knife on the table beside him, and there came a pause and a far-off look in his eyes.

"Oh, father, don't fancy I feel that way—I—don't—I wouldn't think——" began Beverly, eagerly, with a suspicious quaver in his voice. To hide it, he arose suddenly.

"Sit down, son," said Griffith, smiling at the boy and taking the hand that rested on the table. It was cold. He dropped the paper-knife and laid his other hand over his son's. "Beverly, you didn't understand me, I reckon "

—he threw one arm about the boy's shoulders—
"I reckon you didn't understand me. I meant
to say this: I still think my father was wrong.
Now, if I can help it, I don't want the time to
ever come, that when you recall your first independent
effort with me, you will think that
of me. I've always intended to try to remember,
when that time came, to put myself in
your place, and recall my own early struggles—
be nineteen again myself. We will all hate to
have you go so far away. That will be the
hardest part for mother and for all of us; but
if you have thought it all over seriously——"

"I have, indeed, father — for months, and
months. It——"

"Why, all there is to do is for me to look
into the matter and get that stock for you, and
see how we can make the change as easy as possible—as——"

The boy was on his feet. He was struggling
to hide his emotion. Griffith, still holding his
hand, arose. He drew the boy toward him.
Suddenly Beverly understood his father's wish.
He threw both arms about his neck and kissed
him as he had not done since he was a little fel-

low. Mr. Davenport held the boy close to his breast. Beverly was the taller of the two, but the father's form had filled out into portly proportions during these past years and Beverly's was very slight.

"There, there, there!" exclaimed Griffith, presently, blowing a blast upon his handkerchief. "What are we two precious fools crying over? Wasting time! Wasting time! Better go tell your mother all about it and let her get about fixing you up to go. Editor Davenport!" he exclaimed, holding the boy at arm's length. "Well, well, well! what next? Tut, tut, tut, tut! I expect Roy will be wanting to set up a law-office—or a boxing school—in a day or two." Roy's exploit with his fists in behalf of Aunt Judy had always been a family joke. "But, look here, Beverly, I want you to promise me you will be mighty careful to keep out of trouble out there. It's a hot State just now. The times are scorching, and—God only knows what's in store for the country. Keep out of trouble and hasty words, son. Bless me, but I'm glad it's not Roy! He'd be in trouble before he got his first stick set up. They call it a stick, don't they? I'll have to coach up on journalistic language if I'm to have an editor for a son. The proof of the editorials will be in the reading thereof," he added, smiling at the play upon the old saying. "But I stipulate right now that you send me every one you write marked in red, so I won't have to wade through all the other stuff to find yours. If they're as good as that last essay of yours at the Delta, I'll be proud of you, my boy. Only—only don't be too radical! Young blood boils too easy. Mine did. Go slow on this question, Bev. It's bigger than you think it is. In one form or another it has burdened my whole life, and I've never been able to solve it yet—for others, for others. I solved it for myself—as Judy's presence here proves," he added, laughing. Judy's presence and her triumph over the law was a family jest, and Roy's fight on her behalf not wholly a memory of regret.

"He fit fur the ould naiger," remarked the envious Rosanna, from time to time, "but it would be the rear of me loif, shure, before he'd do the same, er even so much as jaw back, fer the loikes o' me!"

CHAPTER XI.

"I'll stand as if a man were author of himself,
And knew no other kin."

Shakespeare.

SINCE Beverly was a Virginian, and since it was well known that at least one of the new owners of the paper was from Massachusetts, it was deemed wise to have Beverly sign all of his editorials where they touched—as they usually did—upon the ever-present, and ever-exciting topic of slave extension. The young fellows were advised by the original owner that the border people were in no mood to accept arguments opposed to the opinions of a large proportion of the property owners, if they supposed these arguments came from persons in any way hostile to their interests—as all the New England people were supposed to be. But, he reasoned, if these arguments came from the pen of one who had known the institution of slavery at its best and had loved the old order of things where it was an established institution and where its roots were, as even Beverly believed, in normal earth and not to be disturbed—if from his pen came the protest against its farther extension—it was believed the natives would accept it in kindness whether they agreed with him or not. Beverly still adhered to the old order of things for the old states. He, like his father, had seen how hard it was to be rid of even a small portion of its power and its responsibility.

At the end of the second year of his new editorial work Beverly had grown to feel himself quite at home with his duties. He had made both friends and enemies. The little office had become the town's center of debate and of political development. The clash of interests had come nearer and nearer. The country was on the eve of an election excitement such as had never before been known. Four parties were in the field. The election of either of the two radical candidates meant civil war beyond hope of evasion. Many still fondly hoped that peace was yet possible if but the compromise candidates were elected. Mr. Davenport held tenaciously to that view. Beverly came out openly against it. If it were staved off by compromise, he insisted that it was only a matter of time when the inevitable would come. He argued that it would be best to meet and settle the issue once and for all.

"I shall cast my first presidential ballot for that Illinois lawyer who flayed Douglas," he wrote to his father. "War is simply inevitable now, and he is a fearless and clear-headed leader. When the extension party sees that he means business, and has the whole North and West behind him the struggle will the sooner be over." But Griffith still hoped for peace and a compromise, and declared his intention to vote for Bell and Everett. "You are simply throwing your vote away," wrote Beverly, insistently, "and after all you have done and suffered because of this thing I am sorry to see you do it, father. I'd rather see you help other people to keep out of the fire that scorched you than to silently allow it to be lighted in the states that are now free—in the new territorial country so soon to be states. But what business have I to advise you? I'm in a position to see it better than you are, is my only excuse. I am going to vote for Lincoln and work for him with all my strength. Things are about as hot as they can be out here, I can tell you. I mail my last editorial on the subject to-day. A good many people here don't half like it, and I've had to buck up to some pretty ugly talk first and last; but--we have to follow our consciences, don't we? That's mine, whether they like it or not. Lots of love to mother and the boys and Margaret—and to Judy, too. And af you plaise, me reshpects t' Rosanna, shure!

"P. S.—I forgot to say I'll have to postpone that visit home for a little while yet, until things settle down a bit. We have all we can possibly manage at the office now. Shap runs the business end of things very well, does the hiring and adv. work and all that. Donaldson takes all the locals and reporting, and I've got pretty much the whole of the editing to do. I sign only the political ones, but I do the other stuff on that page and the literary part too. Of course both of them do some of these things once in a while—and if they want to; but I am depended on for it; so as times are, I've got to be here to meet all these new questions. We talk 'em over and I write 'em up. It keeps me tied, but I like it; I reckon I was born for the business. We are really making great strides for youngsters. The subscriptions have very nearly doubled in the two years. Did you read the issue of the 24th with my lurid remarks on 'Breakers Ahead?' I believe every word of it. I don't believe we are going to pull through without a touch of gunpowder. I don't intend to fight myself, if I can help it—but I shall shoot with ink just as long and as strong as I can. I believe my postscript is a good deal longer than my letter; but sometimes our afterthoughts have more in 'em than the originals, so why not add 'em? I forgot, too, in my gassing about myself, to say how glad I am that Roy is doing so well at college now. I shall surely try to get home to his graduation in June next, for I hope after Lincoln is once in the White House (and you see I assume he is going to get there), that it won't take long to settle matters down. I think by next June I can surely come home for a good visit. I doubt, though, if we do have a place for Roy to take even then. All the places we have to give are rather—well, they are not in his line and the pay is small. The salary list looks pretty big to us on pay-day, but I reckon it looks slim enough to each one of the men who gets his little envelope. Now, I believe that is really all I overlooked replying to in your last : only, once more, father, *do* vote for Lincoln and *don't* throw yourself away on that tinkling little Bell. His chances are hopeless; and if they were not, then the country's chances would be. Might as well just put little Margaret at the helm of a ship. No matter how hard she'd pull, or how sweetly she'd smile or how hard she'd coax, the ship would miss the firm grip needed to steer clear of the breakers. There *are* breakers ahead! Lincoln is our only hope for an undivided country and the limitation, once and for all, of the extension of slavery—*sure, sure.* Again, love to all,

"BEVERLY.

"N. B.—I don't often read my letters over, but if I hadn't read this one I shouldn't be so certain as I am now that if I were my own father and should receive this cock-sure piece of advice from my eldest hopeful, I'd—well, I'd tan him well, verbally. But since I have the good luck to be the eldest of the *very* best and most considerate father in this wide world, I don't expect anything of the kind to happen to me; but if it does, I'll swallow it like a little man—and take my revenge (in a scorching editorial) on some other fellow's father who votes for Bell.

"Meekly,
"B."

Mr. Davenport—as was his habit—read the letter aloud to the family, but he smiled anxiously at Roy's merry comments.

"Beverly is in a bad place to be reckless with his English, just now. That editorial on Breakers Ahead seemed to me to go a good deal too far. I'm glad he says he will not fight if there should be a war—which God forbid."

"I would, then!" remarked Roy. "I'd get up a company right here in college. Lots of the boys declare they'd go."

Mr. Davenport looked at his son over his gold-bowed glasses. There was a suspicious twinkle in his eyes and a twitching of the lips. There was a long pause before he spoke. This son of his had always seemed to Griffith younger than he was.

"How old are you, Roy?" he asked in a spirit of fun. "You'd make a tremendous soldier, now, wouldn't you?—just out of short clothes?"

"I'm older than Bev. was when he left college. I'm twenty. Young men make the best soldiers anyhow. I heard Governor Morton tell you that the last time he was here, and besides——"

"Tut, tut, tut, boy, you attend to your lessons! Twenty! Is that so, Katherine? Is Roy twenty?"

Griffith took his glasses in his hand and held them as if he were trying to magnify the boy in order to see him, and with his other hand tweaked his upper lip as if searching for a mustache. Roy accepted the joke and stretched himself up to his tallest, and from his inch of advantage over his father he put down a patronizing hand on Griffith's head and said, "Bless you, my children, bless you." Griffith changed the direction of his glasses and searched the ceiling with that gratified smile fathers have when they realize that a son really exceeds them in anything. Katherine was laughing at the by-play of the two. Suddenly Griffith turned to his youngest son: "Howard, how old are you? I suppose you will vote this time, and go to war and do no end of great and rash things."

"No, I'll stay at home and nurse the baby. That's the kind of a fellow I am," flung back this petulant one, and the door banged behind him.

"Don't tease Ward," said Katherine. "His temper seems to grow faster than he does just these last two years, and——"

"Highty-tighty! He'd better take a reef in it. If I'd behaved that way with my father he would have prescribed a little hickory oil. How old *is* Howard? Fourteen? Growing too fast by half—but his temper does seem to keep up with the rest of him, I must say. Go and hitch up the century plant, Roy. I want to drive out to the farm. Want to go 'long? Don't. Well, do you, Kath'rine? No? Well, then I guess I'll have to take Margaret. She won't go back on me like that. It'll do her good and she can play with those two peewees of Miller's, while he and I look over the stock and drive about the place a little. Fan's colt was lame the last time I was out. I don't believe the strawberry patch is going to do well this year, either. Did I tell you what a fine fat calf the brindle's is? You'd laugh to see it. It winks at you exactly as if it understood a joke."

The old phaeton—otherwise the "century plant"—dashed up to the door. The combination was especially incongruous. Hitched to it was a great, gray, fiery Arabian stallion. The one-time circuit rider had not lost his love for a good horse, and his little stock farm on the outskirts of the town was the joy of his life. He sadly missed the beautiful valley of his youth, but at least these fields were his. No blue mountains loomed up in the distance, but the beech and maple trees were luxuriant. Mountain stream and narrow pass there were not, but a pebbly brook, in which were minnows, ran through the strip of woods, and Griffith still enjoyed the comradeship of bird and beast and fish. He had named the stallion Selim, after the love of his youth, and no one dared drive him but himself. He took up the lines and called back to Roy as Selim dashed off. "I'll leave Selim and bring Fannie in, so your mother and you can drive to-morrow. 'Bye, Howard! Be a good boy!" he called, as he caught a glimpse of the boy at the corner of the house.

"So'll the devil be a good boy! Just wait till that war comes! They'll see!" he growled, as the "century plant" disappeared. There floated back on the air. "Joy to the world, te, te, tum, tum. Yea, yea, there, Selim! Whoa! Yea! yea! Let earth receive her King! Te, te, tum." The "century plant" and Selim disappeared around the corner, and the fife and drum corps which had startled the horse, drowned all other sounds, and for Howard, all other thoughts. He did not stop to reach the gate. He vaulted over the fence and joined the procession and the refrain of the school-boys who gave words to the music—"on a rail! And we'll ride old Abe, and we'll ride old Abe, and we'll ride him to the White House on a rail!" The boy dropped into the step and the rhythm with a will. He forgot to be sullen.

CHAPTER XII.

" The shears of destiny."—Shakespeare.

War! war! war! The great election was over. The bitterness of faction and of section had only intensified. The inevitable had at last come. Mobs, riots, and confusion followed threats, and at last the shot that struck Fort Sumter echoed in every village and hamlet in the country. The beginning of the struggle with arms to adjust the differences between two irreconcilable doctrines—two antagonistic social and economic policies—had culminated. The adjustment must, indeed, now come. "Seventy-five thousand troops for three months!" The President's call rang out, and almost before the echo died away the quota was full. The young, the adventurous, and the hot-headed, supplemented the patriotic and sprang into line. To these it was to be a three months' camping-out lark. Of course the South would back down at the show of armed strength and firm resistance to disunion. The martial spirit, the fighting instinct inherent in the race—that legacy from our brute ancestry—was fanned into flame like fire in a summer wind. College classes were depleted. Young lads hastened to force themselves into the ranks. Drum and fife and bugle sounded in every street. LeRoy Davenport was one of the first to enlist. The company of college boys elected him their second lieutenant, and they left at once for Camp Morton to be ready to march to the front at the first order for troops from the west. He looked very fine and soldierly and handsome in his uniform, and with the straps upon his shoulders. Beverly wrote that he should stick to his editorial chair. He slept in the office, to be ready to receive and write up every scrap of news the moment it came. He wrote a series of fiery editorials, denouncing the "outrage on the flag at Fort Sumter." An anonymous letter was pushed under his office-door warning him to desist. He published the letter and appended to it a more vigorous article than before. That night, as he lay on the bed in the little back room of the office, he thought he detected a strange odor. He went softly to the window and looked out. The moon was just rising on the river. His little row-boat, in which his fishing and pleasure trips were taken, bobbed idly up and down on the waves just under the corner of the building. The strange odor grew stronger and more distinct in character. He began to suspect that he understood it. He opened the door into the front room and passed on to the compositors' room. He was sure now that it was the smell of smoke and oil-soaked cloth. His first impulse was to open the front door and shout fire, but he remembered Lovejoy's fate and paused. He stepped to the front window and turned the old slats of the heavy green blinds so that he could see out into the narrow street. There were three forms crouching near the door. He thought he saw the gleam of steel. Flames had begun to creep under the door and from the compositors' room. Suddenly the flimsy pine partition burst into a sheet of flame. He knew that to open the front door was to meet death at the hands of desperadoes. He caught up the only implement of defense he saw—a pair of great, sharp, clipping-shears, and started for the door. He intended, at least, to mark his man so that others could deal with him afterward. Suddenly he remembered that he could drop from the back window into the river. If they had not taken his oars he could escape. The room was as light as day now, and he knew that to hesitate was to be lost. He dropped the curious weapon he had in his hand, and ran to the back room. The only rope there was the support of the old-fashioned bed. He hastily unwound it and fastened it to the bed-post nearest the window. He wanted to make the drop as short as possible, lest the splash of the water attract the men from the front of the house. He smiled when he climbed into the boat and found the oars safely in its bottom. In an instant he was pulling gently, softly, slowly out into the stream. He could almost hear the beating of his own heart. Then in the moonlight a shot rang out on the clear air, and a sharp crack, as the ball struck the side of the boat, told him that he was discovered. No need for caution now! Need only for haste and strength! He pulled with all his young vigor

—with the stroke of an accustomed hand. The sky was livid with the flames from his burning office—the dream and hope of his first manhood was melting before his eyes. "God damn 'em!" he said, between his set teeth, as two more shots followed him, "they won't dare stay longer now —and I'm out of range. God damn 'em!" He let the oars fall by his side. He could see numbers of men running about now, shouting, swearing, vainly trying to check the flames. Some one yelled, "Shoot again, he's in that skiff!"

He heard and understood that the victim was being made out the culprit. The would-be assassins were covering retreat. He decided that it would not be safe to pull back to the Missouri side just then. He would land on the Kansas shore. Morning found him near a small village. He landed and made his way directly to the newspaper office. It was one of his own exchanges, and a free-soil paper like his. He told his story, and the editor made a lurid article out of it and called for his townsmen to gather in a public meeting. He issued an extra, and Beverly was the hero of the hour. Rough frontiersmen—some of whom had seen his paper—looked at the slender stripling and volunteered to cross the river and "clean out the town." They called on Beverly for a speech. They were bent upon making him a leader. The war fever was in the frontier blood. He began his speech in a passion of personal feeling, but ended in an appeal for volunteers, "not to fight *my* battle, not to avenge my wrong, not to repair my loss, but to fight this great battle for liberty and freedom in the great northwest! It seems we will have to fight for the freedom of speech and press, as well as for free soil! I will be frank: I had not intended to enlist in this war. I had hoped to do more good by argument than I could hope to do by arms. I had hoped to see the end of it at the end of the three months for which the President called for troops; but I do not stand on that ground any longer. Yesterday, as you all know, there was issued a new call for five hundred thousand more men! I want, now, to be one of the first of those, and I shall enlist for three years or for ten years or as long as this war lasts; and I don't want to come out of it alive if I have got to come out into a country where free speech is throttled and a free press burned up! I shall enlist, I tell you, and since I had to fly to Kansas for protection, I hope that Kansas will enroll me as *her* son, and if it may be, as her very first volunteer!"

The idea took the fancy of his listeners. "Raise a regiment!" "I'll go with you!" "Three cheers for the editor!"

They were given with a will, and the enthusiasm for himself put a new idea into his head.

"I am only twenty-three years old," he said laughing, "and not much bigger than the right arm of some of you great, fine, muscular fellows; but if you are willing to trust me, I would ask nothing better than to take the lead of such a body of men. If enough of you will enlist here and now, I'll go with you as private or as captain. I'll take the lead and the responsibility, or I'll follow any better qualified man you may name, and we'll go up to the capital and offer ourselves as the first Kansas volunteers for this war!"

Almost before he had spoken the words cheer after cheer rent the air. Men signified their willingness to enlist, and before night on the first day he had spent on Kansas soil he found himself marching toward the capital at the head of one hundred determined, rough, strong, fearless frontiersmen to ask for a commission as their captain, and for arms and ammunition for his men.

Mr. Davenport was surprised that day to receive this dispatch :

"Am elected Captain, Company A, First Kansas Vols. Will write.

"BEVERLY."

They could not imagine at home why Beverley should be in a Kansas company, but when the *Gazette* came that night with an account of the burning of the obscure newspaper-office out in Missouri, they understood, and Katherine felt faint and sick when she realized that two of her boys had gone to fight against her people. She knew that her own brothers and nephews would all be on the other side, and that Griffith's were there too. Griffith had gone with Roy's company to Camp Morton and had sorrowfully consented to his enlistment; but if war there must be and if his son must go, Griffith felt that he was on the right side. He held back, himself, from the idea that fighting was necessary, even yet. At the very worst, it would all be over very soon, he thought, and he hoped and believed that a few demonstrations of determination on the part of the Government would undoubtedly settle the matter without any real or serious fighting. He was unalterably opposed to a division of the Union, and he believed that the South would see its mistake on that question and reconsider it. But as State after State seceded, his perplexity deepened. He and Katherine had all these years kept up a fond and constant correspondence with the old home friends and kinsmen, several of whom, from time to time, had visited them. All these had felt that Griffith had made a grievous mistake in following the course he had taken, but until now no real bitterness had resulted. Now, all letters ceased. They had heard, somehow, in the old home, that Griffith's sons had enlisted in the Union army—to fight against them! That was more than they could bear. Even before the line of communication was finally closed against letters, theirs had ceased to come—and Katherine understood. Many a night she sobbed herself to sleep.

"How terrible this all is, Griffith! How terrible! Why should they fight over it? Why don't they let the slave states go, if they want to, and be one government, and the others be free states and another government—as Canada and we are, or as Mexico and we?"

Griffith had tried to explain the difficulties and the inevitable clashing of interests that would be forever resulting—the constant and eternal clashing. He pointed out that no country would allow itself to be divided. He read to her long arguments in support of the maintenance of the Union; but she said:

"Yes, I see it is desirable if all want it so; but if they do *not*, why—why—I wouldn't fight to compel them to stay with me if they want to go. You never do that way with your children, Griffith, you know you don't. You never did try to conquer one of them and force him to think your way. You always felt that way about freeing the slaves, too. You said you did not judge for other people—only for yourself. And when you saw how terribly hard it was to do it, and that most people could not do as you did even if they wanted to—you always said that you did not blame them in the least."

"I say so yet. I know all that; but governments are very different. Some one has got to decide for others. If they didn't, everything would go to smash in very short order. I suppose I am a good deal of a coward. I can't bear to judge for other people. But I do believe in maintaining this government at any and all cost—but I'd leave slavery alone in the South. I wouldn't let it spread. That is Lincoln's policy now. He said so in his message—his inaugural. If it will stay where it is, he says he won't disturb it—and that suits me; but if it will not——"

"Well, it won't," put in Howard. "I heard Governor Morton say so in his speech last night. He said that this fight had all along been really to extend and not to retain slavery, and when that was lost then the South proposed to smash the Union. That's exactly what he said; but, 'We'll rally round the flag, boys, we'll rally once again,'" he sang, and banged the door behind him.

That night Howard disappeared. He had run away, sworn that he was eighteen years old and enlisted under another name, as a gunner in a battery! It was ten days before a trace of him was found. Then he was on his way to the front whence news had come thick and fast of skirmishes, battles and tremendous preparations for a terrible and bloody struggle. Excitement was at fever heat. The streets were crowded with soldiers and echoed with martial music night and day. War, indeed, was upon them, and fair July was here.

CHAPTER XIII.

THE OTHER SIDE OF WAR.

In Washington, on the twentieth of July, 1861, expectation ran high. A decisive, and it was hoped a final blow was to be struck on the following day. Large numbers of troops had passed through the city and been massed thirty miles away. A great battle was imminent. Both armies had recently won small victories. Both were jubilant. For the most part the soldiers in these two opposing camps were raw recruits. They sang and joked and played tricks on each other. To both, war was a mere name yet, a painted glory, a sabred, gold-laced parade before admiring, cheering crowds. The Confederates knew every step of the ground. To their opponents it was an unknown land into which they had been marched; rugged, broken country, the like of which the most of them had never before seen. Raw and untried they were on both sides, but the lack of knowledge of the topography—of the location of pass and defile, of ford and of stream—gave to the Union troops (when they had deigned to think of it at all) a certain feeling of insecurity and uneasiness. Still no one doubted for a moment the outcome. The battle would be fought and won, and glory would be carried home on every Union bayonet. Civilians drove out to camp from the city, and from distant hilltops were prepared to witness the battle. A martial display like this may not be seen through field-glasses every day. Early in the day cannonading had been heard. More citizens started for the scene of action. There were intervals of comparative silence, and then again the boom of cannon and the rattle of muskets told the distant audience that hostilities were on—that neither side had finally yielded. Later a number of citizens drove furiously across the Long Bridge with the news that the Northern troops were retreating toward the city. Then word came that they had rallied, but citizens deserted their posts of observation and rode rapidly toward town. They reported the

Southern troops as fighting fiercely, but it was thought they were about to yield. They could not hold out much longer against the murderous fire of the Union men. Suddenly a flying horseman with livid face and white lips sped through the streets. It was a messenger from the front! He was making straight to the White House! The Northern troops were in full retreat! People looked at each other in dismay. Surely they would rally! They would not come to the city! They were only falling back! They would form and attack again! People told each other these things and turned pale. The streets began to be filled with returning civilians. No one stopped. Every one pushed on toward home or to the Capitol. Another foam-flecked horse dashed in. The rider had on a uniform, dirty, begrimed and wet.

"The Northern troops have broken ranks! They are fleeing, horse and foot, in one mass of disorganized panic-stricken humanity, pursued by a murderous fire from a jubilant, victory-intoxicated enemy! The officers could not rally them! It is a panic!" No need to question the facts. Look at the distant hills. Watch the approaches. See the succession of dispatch bearers fly past to the White House! "It is only a retreat! They will rally!" called back one rider only to be contradicted by the next. "It is not a retreat! It is a panic! They have broken ranks. Men are flying madly. Guns, ammunition, everything that hinders speed have been thrown away! Each man is flying to save himself! Washington is in danger!"

The climax had indeed come. The dismay knew no bounds. What next? Must the President escape? Where should he go? If he left, what could Congress do? Must all fly? Where? Would the enemy invade Washington? Was the Northern army really so disorganized, so demoralized? In the name of God! what could it all mean? People all asked questions. There was no one to answer them—no one but the stragglers who began to come in. Were the brave fellows who had so gallantly and cheerfully marched out not brave after all? Were they outnumbered? Were there no reinforcements? What was the solution? They had not long to wait. A handful of horsemen, shame-faced and hesitant, then worn out and hard-driven teams began to appear at the far end of the Long Bridge. All Washington took to its housetops. Anxious faces watched for some approaching line. None came; but the Long Bridge was gorged with a struggling mass of horse, foot and ordnance. There was no pretense of a line of march. Each man fled by and for himself. Twilight saw the streets filled with men in soiled and torn uniform; uniform which had but just marched out fresh and resplendent. Sullen replies greeted questions.

"By God, we didn't know where we were! Officers didn't know any more'n we did."

"Had us in a pocket!"

"Gad, we was *lost*—didn't know the way in *ner* out! Try it yerself."

"Willin' t' fight—but not willin' t' go it blind like that." Ambulances, limping footmen, infantry, cavalry, ordinance and supply wagons crowded and jostled and swore and cursed each at the other. Each struggled for place in advance. The Long Bridge, the Aqueduct Bridge, the

Chain Bridge, all were one mad scene of confusion. The terrified men saw the dome of the Capitol and their aim was to reach it by the nearest route. The thought of the unknown country had been to them a nightmare from which escape was their only desire. All night the ghastly spectacle was kept up. No one slept. No one knew what to expect on the morrow. Would the city be bombarded from the heights beyond? Would it be shelled and burned? Would these panic-stricken men rally? Could they be depended upon, or was the fright now so in their blood that they would refuse to form in line again and obey commands? Could they be relied upon? Pennsylvania avenue was lined with tired, terrified, and wounded men. Churches were turned into hospitals. Nobody slept. Surgeons were everywhere. More wounded kept coming in. Surgeons from Baltimore, from Philadelphia, and even from New York responded to telegrams. Special trains rushed in. Washington was one mad whirl of fright and dismay! Next morning the whole country was electrified by the terrible news. "Extra! 'stra! 'stro!

Extra! all 'bout terrible defeat m-m-m-'ion troops! 'stra! 'stra! 'stro!'" In every town and hamlet in the country—on every table there was spread the awful news on the morning of July 22. Men began to take on another look. This, indeed, was serious! What was to be done? Reserve troops were started without delay from camp and home. Excitement was at fever heat. Would the fresh troops arrive in time? Could Washington hold out? Must the President fly? Another kind of question bore hard upon many a household. Who was killed? Who wounded? Who missing? People looked into each other's eyes and feared to ask or to speak of this question nearest their hearts.

Roy Davenport's regiment was ordered to the front. Henceforth camp life would be no picnic. They could be boys no longer. Men were needed at the front. Beverly's company had some time since joined the troops in the Southwest and was in the field. The battery in which Howard acted as gunner was with Sherman in the far South. For the first time the seriousness of the situation was borne home to the whole

North. To feel that Washington was really in danger gave a new meaning to defeat. Why had the Northern troops met such a fearful disaster? Before this they had won in almost every contest, but this was worth all the rest to the South so near was it to Washington—so near to Richmond. The two capitals faced each other like gladiators, and the first serious blow had fallen with crushing force upon the Union champions. If Washington fell the Confederacy was sure of foreign recognition—of success.

Griffith had a long talk with Governor Morton when he went to see Roy's regiment off. When he came home he was pale and anxious. There was a new trouble on his heart. He did not tell Katherine that Morton had urged him to volunteer his services to the Government as a guide through the passes and defiles of his native State.

"Your knowledge of that country would be simply invaluable. It would prevent any such disaster as this again. Panics like this ruin an army. It will take months to recover from such a rout even if nothing worse comes of it. The moral effect is simply fatal. You are a Union man and you know every foot of that country. Our generals don't. They are afraid to risk getting their men into a pocket and losing their whole command. You can help. The main battle-ground is bound to be Virginia; we can accomplish nothing of value until we know and feel secure on that soil—until the State is an open book to us. Let me wire the President that you will. Let——"

Griffith held up his hand.

"I cannot! I cannot!" he said. "It is my old State; I love it and my people. I have done enough for my country. I have done my share. I have given my property, my friends, my home, and now my three boys—all, all I have given for my conscience and my country's sake. Surely I have done my whole duty, I will not betray my State! I will not!"

Over and over the Governor had returned to the attack only to receive the same reply. Day after day he argued with Griffith, and still ill news came from the front. The army of the Potomac seemed paralyzed after its repulse. The real gravity of the situation was, for the first time, borne in upon both the military and the political mind. If the great foreign powers recognized the Confederate government, the Republic was lost. If Washington fell, that recognition was assured—and still "all was quiet on the Potomac."

The middle of July the wires had flashed the news of the defeat of the Confederates at Boonville, Missouri, by Lyons' men. Beverly had been there, and had written the full account home. Then he was at Carthage, and was full of fight and enthusiasm. After his account of the battle at Carthage, he had other things to tell. "I didn't get a scratch either place, but the day after the last fight I did get a lot of fun out of it. I suppose you won't be able to see how there could be any fun in the situation. Well, I'll tell you one or two things. One of my men showed the white feather, and we were thinking of court-martialing and making an example of him. I made up my mind to give Hartman (that was the fellow's name, Bill Hartman) a chance to tell me privately his side of the story. Says I, 'Bill, I've asked all your neighbors here in camp if you were a coward at home, and they all say you were not only brave, but you had proved it many a time. Now, I want to save you this court-martial if I can, and I want you to tell me your side of it. How did it happen?'

"'Well,' said he, transferring his quid of tobacco to his other cheek, 'Cap, it's this a-way. I can't seem t' jest stand right up an' shoot a feller I ain't had no words with. I want to pick out my man when I kill him, an' I want t' kinder have a quah'l with him fust. I can't seem t' jest stand right up an' kill a man I ain't had *no* words with. I can't do it, somehow er 'nother, Cap.'

"I don't know how I'm going to manage to get Bill into a 'quah'l' with some special Reb before the next fight, and then make sure he'll get a chance to pop at that particular one in action! We'll have to get up some scheme, I suppose. Bill is too good a soldier to be hampered and to have his usefulness impaired by a simple want of a feeling of personal revenge! I reckon if the truth were told, though, we all fight a good deal better if we have that stimulant. Another ludicrous thing happened the other day. I was sent out, just with an orderly, to see if I could learn anything of the movements of the enemy. We had on citizens' clothes, and we jogged along until we were within field-glass distance of Harris's camp. He is an old West Pointer and a tactician. I've heard that they call him 'Old Logistics and Strategy'—and I must say if his advice in the Senate had been followed last winter we'd have had a mighty poor show here now. But when we got where we thought we could see something, quite a shower came up and our glass was no use. Under the cover of the rain I ventured a good deal closer; and, if you'll believe me, his command were sitting on their horses, drawn up in line, with umbrellas raised! The absurdity of the thing nearly knocked my pins from under me. I only wished I could get near enough to see the effect on Old Logistics when he should emerge from his tent—and he a West Pointer! But you don't need to make any mistakes about their fighting—these natives. We've found that they will fight to the death, but they've got their own ideas on the subject of soldiering in the meantime. Most of 'em carry their powder in a pouch, and it needs to be

kept dry! It was the very funniest thing I ever
saw, though. The rain came down in such torrents
I couldn't get an idea how many there
were, but, from the way they fought us next day,
I made up my mind there must be pretty close
to a million—and they didn't use umbrellas to
protect themselves, either! They took our storm
of shot cooler than they did the rain in camp,
and they fought like demons. Of course, their
equipments don't compare with ours. Most of
them have their old home guns—no two alike.
But a good lot of our boys are carrying around
some of their ammunition inside of them just
now, all the same. One of the prisoners we
took—a straggler—told us that none of his
command are regularly enlisted. They are
afraid to enlist; say that Old Logistics is a
'reg'lar,' and, if they enlist and then don't
do just his way, he'll court-martial them.
They argue that, if they don't regularly enlist,
he can't do anything to them. They are ready
and eager to fight, but they don't propose to
be subject to 'regular' discipline in the intervals.
This fellow says half of the command
go home nights—to their farms and stores—and

return at dawn the next morning. I think he is lying about the numbers who do, but I don't doubt that some do. He vows he is telling the cold fact. Fancy the humor of commanding an army under umbrellas, who go home nights to milk the cows! But undertake to fight 'em, and there is no laugh left. That is not their comic side. We have orders to move in the morning and are all ready. I will let you hear again the moment we stop."

Before this letter of Beverly's reached home the telegraphic news of the battle of Wilson's Creek filled the papers. Beverly's name appeared among the wounded: "Seriously, not fatally—Captain Beverly Davenport; shot in three places while covering retreat after General Lyon fell. Young Captain Davenport's men did good service. His command lost heavily." No further news came. Griffith telegraphed, but could get no reply.

"You must go and bring him home," said Katherine. "I cannot bear this suspense any longer."

She had grown pale and hollow-eyed in these few days of anxiety. Griffith went. He found

Beverly doing well, but a ball had gone through his sword-arm and two others were imbedded in his flesh. His horse had fallen beneath him and he had had to walk on the wounded leg, and had lost much blood. He looked weak and thin. His orderly had written home for him, but the letter had never come. Griffith urged him to go home and recuperate, but he would not listen to the proposition. Griffith wrote home to Katherine and then waited. The command was ordered to move, and still Beverly was not able to go with it. The commander ordered him to go home until able to report for duty.

He was a sensation in the village. He was the first handsome young wounded officer to return. Alas! they were plenty enough later on; but now his limp and his arm suspended in a sling made him a hero, indeed. Many were the demonstrations in his honor. The Governor came to see him, and strove again to convince Griffith that he, too, was needed at the front. "I have told President Lincoln about you," he said. "You can see for yourself what the army in Virginia is doing ever since Bull Run—

nothing at all. Those two defeats—Buil Run and Ball's Bluff—stopped them off entirely. Action that will be effective is simply impossible without knowing the lay of the land. Northern men don't know it, and we can't trust Southern men to tell the truth, of course, about it. The rebels know that perfectly well, and they bank on it. They keep their best and strongest generals, and men who know the State like a book, right there between Washington and Richmond. It won't do to let it be generally known, for that would put panic into our troops when they are tried next; but there is not a soul the President can trust who knows those passes and defiles and fords. Captain, I hope you know them. I don't believe *you* will refuse to go any place you are needed. As a recruit—an enlisted man—you *can't* refuse."

"Go," said Beverly; "go! why of course I would if I knew the country as father does, but I don't. You see father used to be a circuit-rider. He knows every foot of it as if it were his front yard, but I would know only a few miles near where we lived. I was only a boy then. It is a hard country to learn. Passes are many and blind. Fords change—it takes a native and an expert to feel safe with them. If I——" He turned suddenly to his father in his enthusiasm. "Why don't you go, father? If the President wants you—if your country needs you, why——" He saw the look that crept into his father's face, and he understood. The young fellow limped to his father's side and laid his left hand on his shoulder.

"Father has done enough," he said, looking at the Governor. "Do not ask him to do this. He fought his battle before the North came to it. He has borne and suffered enough, Governor. Father is a Virginian, blood, bone, and ancestry. He loves his people and his old home. We boys don't remember it as he does, but to him—to him, it will always be home. They will always be his people."

"Unless it is desperate and I am ordered, I shall not go," said Griffith, looking up almost defiantly. "You need not ask me again, Governor. I have done my share. I have done more for my country and my conscience than many men will be called upon to do—I have done my share."

The Governor gave it up, but he did not forget one phrase, " unless it is desperate—unless I am ordered." That night he started for Washington, and a week later Beverly returned to his command and to duty in the field.

CHAPTER XIV.

A SILENT HERO.

One evening Griffith sat by the library table reading, and Katherine was moving about the room restlessly. For several days no news had come from the front—no home news, no letters from the absent sons. The door leading to the porch was open and suddenly there stood before them a messenger with a telegram. Katherine grew weak and sick. Griffith tore the envelope open and read. She watched his face. Every vestige of blood had left it, and his head sank on his arms crossed on the table before him. The telegram was crushed in one hand. A groan escaped him, and then a sob shook his frame.

"Which one is it? Which one of my boys is killed? Which—which one?" cried Katherine. She tried to loosen the hand that clasped the message, but he held it crushed, and when he lifted his head tears were streaming down his cheeks. He tried to reassure her. "It is not *that*," he said, hoarsely. "They—the boys are all right, but they have ordered me——." He relaxed his grasp, and his head sank again on his arms.

She took the message and read:

"Washington, D. C.
"Report here immediately.
"A. Lincoln."

For a moment Katherine seemed stunned. She did not comprehend. Then she seemed to rise far above her normal stature.

"*You shall not go!*" she said. Her eyes blazed. Her hands hung by her sides, but they were clenched until the nails sank into the flesh. The tigress in her was at last aroused. "You shall *not* go! How dare he? With three of my boys in the army now! With us reduced to *this!*" She had never complained of the change in her style of living, but she flung out the contemptuous fire within her as she stretched out her arms to indicate the simplicity of her surroundings. "With *this* in exchange for what we had! With every tie broken! With every luxury and comfort gone! Separated from even the negroes that loved us and begged to come with us! How *dare* they ask for further sacrifice from us! How dare he!"

Griffith's head lifted slowly. He looked at her in dismay. Was this the patient, compliant wife who had willingly given up her fortune and her home to satisfy *his* conscience? Was this the silent, demure, self-controlled Katherine— this very tall, angry woman? She looked like a fury unchained. She took a step nearer to him.

"You shall *not* go!" she repeated, and the astonished messenger-boy fled in affright, as she suddenly threw both arms about Griffith and began to sob convulsively.

Griffith held her to his breast, which heaved and choked him. It seemed to him that he could not speak. At last he whispered softly: "I must go, Katherine. It is an order from the President. I will have to go to Washington." He had not finished speaking until he felt her form begin to shrink and collapse in his grasp.

Her eyes half closed, half opened again, then closed and a ghastly pallor spread itself over her face. For the first time in her life Katherine had fainted. His first thought was that she was dead. A great wave of fear and then of self-reproach swept over him. He sat staring in the ghastly face.

"I have sacrificed her very life to my conscience," he moaned aloud. "I had no right to do that! God help me! God forgive me! What *is* it right to do? Can we *never* know what is right?" He was holding her in his arms, with his own face upturned and staring eyes. "God help me! God help me! What *is* it right to do?" he moaned again.

"'Fo' de good Lawd on high, Mos' Grif, what de matter wif Mis' Kate? What de mattah wif all two, bofe of yoh?" exclaimed Aunt Judy. "I done see dat little rapscallion what brung de telegraf letter run fo' deah life, an' he yell back dat Mis' Kate done gone crazy, an'——"

Judy had hobbled to his side, and her old eyes were growing used to the changed light. She saw his tear-stained face and Katherine's lifeless form in his arms.

"Is Mis' Kate daid, Mos' Grif?" she asked, in an awed voice.

"I have killed her," he said, like one in a dream, looking at the old woman as to one who could be relied on to understand. Katherine's eyelids began to move. They slowly lifted and closed again. The old woman saw it first.

"Mos' Grif, wat fo' yoh tell me dat kine er talk? Mis' Kate, she ain't daid. She's des foolin'. Yoh ain't hu'tted, is yoh, honey?" she cooed, stroking Katherine's hair. "Nobody ain't hu'tted yoh, is dey, Mis' Kate? Nobody——"

"Get some water—quick, quick!" said Griffith, and struggled to the couch with his burden. He knelt beside her and stroked her forehead and chafed her hands. He could not speak, but he tried to control his distorted features, that she might not understand—might not remember—when she should open her eyes.

"Heah some wattah, honey. Des yoh take a big sup. Hit gwine ter do yoh good. Dar, now, I gwine ter lif' yoah haid. Now, den, yoh des lay des dat away, an' Aunt Judy gwine ter run an' git dat rabbit foot! Dat gwine ter cuah yoh right off. It is dat. Dey ain't no doctah in dis roun' worl' kin cuah yoh like wat dat kin— let erlone one er dese heah Yankee doctahs! Hit fotch me to you alls dat time wat yoh runned away, an' hit fetch dem roses back to yoah cheeks, too. Dat hit kin!"

She hobbled off to her loft to find her precious talisman, and Griffith softly closed and locked the door behind her. Katherine lay so still he thought she had fallen asleep. He could see her breathing. He went to his seat beside the couch and gently fanned her pale face. The color had come again in the lips. Presently he went softly across the room and took up the crumpled message from the floor, where she had dropped it.

"Report here immediately.

"A. LINCOLN."

There could be no mistake about that. It was a command from the President, imperative, urgent. He sank into the chair again, and his head fell on his folded arms on the table. His lips were moving, but there was no sound. At last he was conscious of a light tapping on the window. He was surprised to find that it was dark. He crossed the room to find Rosanna outside with a tray.

"Shure, an' Oi troied both dures, an' not a sound did Oi git. 'Tis long phast yer tay toime, an' not a pick have ye et—nayther wan av yez. The ould nayger's done fed the baby an' put her t' bed. Shure, an' she's a-galavantin' 'round here thryin' the dures an' windeys, flourishin' the fut av a bunnie, be jabbers! She says 'tis what yez wants fer yer health; but, sez Oi, *viddles* is what they wants, sez Oi—an' here they be."

Griffith opened the door.

"Is it wan av the young maisthers kilt, shure?" she whispered, as she put the tray down.

Griffith shook his head.

"Well, thanks be t' Almoighty God an' all the blished saints! Oi feared me it was the young maisther—an' shure an' ye'd go fur and not foind the loikes av *him* agin. He looked just simply ghrand in his ossifer's uni*forum*. Yez moight say ghrand! Shure an' nobody else could match up wid 'im! He looked that rehspectable! An' the schape av 'im!" She threw up her hands and admired the absent Beverly. "The schape av 'im! Yez moight say! He shurely do become them soger close! Now, can't yez ate the rear av thim berries, dear? They're simply ghrand, they're shplendid!"

Katherine seemed to be sleeping, and Griffith soon pushed the tray aside. Rosanna took it up. Then she leaned forward.

"Shure, an' that ould nayger's awful rehspectable; ye can see that by the lukes av her; but she's thet foolish with her ould ded bunnie fut thet she makes me craipy in me shpine."

She glanced about her before venturing out, and then made a sudden dash for the kitchen.

CHAPTER XV.

"The depths and shoals of honor." *Shakespeare.*

WHEN Griffith reached Washington he sent his name directly to the President, and was told to go to the room which Mr. Lincoln called his workshop, and where his maps were. The walls and tables were covered with them. There was no one in the room when Griffith entered. He walked to a window and stood looking out. In the distance, across the river, he could see the heights. He noticed a field-glass on the table. He took it up and focused it. The powerful instrument seemed to bring the Long Bridge to his very feet. He remembered in what tense excitement he had seen and crossed that bridge last, and how he had thought and spoken of it as the dead-line. He recalled the great relief he had felt when his negroes and his own carriage had at last touched free soil—were indeed in the streets of Washington. It came over him that the country, as well as he, had traveled a very long way since that time—and over a stormy road. A blare of martial music sounded in the distance. He watched the soldiers moving about in parade. He thought of his own sons, and wondered where they were and if they were all safe to-day. A heavy sigh escaped him, and a hand fell upon his shoulder. He turned to face the tall, strange, dark man who had entered so silently. His simple and characteristically direct words were not needed to introduce him. No one could ever mistake the strong face that had been caricatured or idealized by friend or foe in every corner of the land, but which, after all, had never been reproduced with its simple force and rugged grandeur. Before Griffith could speak he felt that the keen but kindly eyes had taken his measure—he was being judged by a reader of that most difficult, varied and complicated of languages—the language of the human face.

"I am Abraham Lincoln," he said, as if he were introducing a man of but slight importance, "and you are Mr. Davenport. I was expecting you." He took Griffith's hand and shook it warmly, in the hearty, western fashion, which, in Mr. Lincoln's case, had also a personal quality of frankness and of a certain human longing for that contact of the real with the real which it is the function of civilization to wipe out.

"I would have known you any place, Mr. Lincoln," began Griffith. "Your pictures——"

"Anybody would," broke in the President, with his inimitable facial relaxation, which was not a smile, but had in it a sense of humor struggling to free it from its somber cast, "anybody would. My pictures are ugly enough, but none of 'em ever did my ugliness full justice, but then they never look like anybody else. I remember once, out in Sangamon county, I said if ever I saw a man who was worse looking than I, I'd give him my jack-knife. The knife was brand new then."

He ran his hand through his stiff, black hair and gave it an additional air of disorder and stubbornness. He had placed a chair for Griffith and taken one himself. He crossed one long leg over the other and made a pause.

Griffith was waiting for the end of his story.

He concluded that there was to be no end, and he ventured a quizzical query:

"You don't mean to tell me that you are carrying that knife yet, Mr. President?"

Both laughed. Griffith felt strangely at home already with this wonderful man. He did not realize that it was this particular aim which had actuated Mr. Lincoln from the moment he had entered the room. This reader and leader of men had taken the plan of his legal years, and was taking time to analyze his guest while he threw him off his guard. In the midst of the laugh he stretched out his long leg and dived into his trousers' pocket.

"No, sir, you may not believe it, but that's not the same knife! I carried the other one—well—I reckon it must have been as much as fifteen years—with that offer open. It lost its beauty—and I didn't gain mine. It was along in the fifties somewhere, when one day I was talking with a client of mine on the corner of the main street in Springfield, and along came a fellow and stopped within ten feet of us. I looked at him and he looked at me, and we both looked into a looking-glass in the store window.

I'd tried to be an honorable man all my life, and hard as it was to part with an old friend, I felt it was my duty to give him that knife—and I did."

There was a most solemn expression on his host's face. Griffith laughed heartily again. The President was gazing straight before him.

"I don't know where that man came from, and I don't know where he went to, but he won that knife fair and square. I was a good deal of a beauty compared to him!"

The very muscles of his face twinkled with humor. No one would have felt the homeliness of his face, lit as it now was in its splendid ruggedness, with the light and glory of a great and tender soul playing with its own freaks of fancy.

But before the laugh had died out of Griffith's voice, the whole manner of the President had changed. He had opened the pen-knife and was drawing the point of the blade down a line on the large map which lay on the table beside him.

"Morton tells me that you used to be a circuit-rider down in these mountains here, and that you know every pass, defile and ford in the

State." He looked straight at Griffith and ran his great, bony hand over his head and face, but went hastily on: "I know how that is myself. Used to be a knight of the saddlebags out in Illinois, along about the same time—only my circuit was legal and yours was clerical. I carried Blackstone in my saddlebags—after I got able to own a copy—and you had a Bible. I reckon—volumes of the law in both cases! Let me see. How long ago was that?"

"I began in twenty-nine, Mr. President, and rode circuit for ten years. Then I was located and transferred the regular way each one or two years up to fifty-three. That—year—I—left—my—native—state."

Mr. Lincoln noticed the hesitancy in the last words, the change in the tone, the touch of sadness. He inferred at once that what Senator Morton had told him of this man's loyalty had had something to do with his leaving the old home.

"Found it healthier for you to go West, did you? Traveled toward the setting sun. Wanted to keep in the daylight as long as you could; but I see you took the memory of the dear old home with you. Have you never been back?"

"I don't look like much of an outlaw, do I, Mr. Lincoln?" asked Griffith, with a sad smile.

"Can't say I would take you for one, no." The President turned a full, long, searching look upon him.

"Well, I have never been back—home—I— I left two freed slaves in the State when I came away, and, you know——"

Mr. Lincoln laughed for the first time aloud. "Ha, ha, ha, ha, ha! You remind me of a case we had out in Illinois. There was an old fellow trying to stock a pond he had with fish. Well, that pond was so close to town and so handy, that the boys—some of 'em about as old as you and me—caught 'em out as fast as he put 'em in. By and by his son got into the Legislature, and one day when there wasn't a great deal of other law to make or to spoil, he got the other members to vote for a bill to punish anybody for taking anything out of that pond. His bill said, 'for fishing anything out of that pond.' Well, one day a little son of his fell in and got so far from shore before they saw him that they had to literally fish him out with a pole. Some of the fishermen around there wanted him arrested for violation of the law he had passed to hit them. —Fact! He and you are about the same sort of criminals." He turned to the map again. "Of course I understand what you mean. Yes, yes, I know. These very passes and fords are dear to you. Some people have that sort of attachments. I have. Why, I'd feel like getting down off o' my horse at many a place out on my old circuit and just making love to the very earth beneath my feet! O, I know how you feel! These old fords are old friends. As you rode along at another place, certain thoughts came to you, and kept you company for miles. They would come back to you right there again. Right over there was a sorrowful memory. You knew the birds that nested in this defile, and you stopped and put the little fellows back in the nest when they had fallen out—and they were not afraid of you. I know how that is. They never were afraid of me—none but the yellow-legged chickens." He smiled in his quizzical way. He was still testing and studying his guest, while keeping him off his guard, and making him forget the President in his relations with the man.

Griffith had begun to wonder how he could know about those birds and woodland friends of long ago, but the yellow-legged chicken joke was so familiar to the preacher that he smiled absently, as in duty bound.

"I'm really glad to know that there are other circuit-riders than we of the cloth who strike terror to the inmates of the barnyard, but I never before heard any one else accused of it."

"I remember, once," began Mr. Lincoln, recrossing his long legs and taking up the penknife again—"I remember, once, when a lot of us were riding over to a neighboring town from Springfield. I had the wrong end of a case, I know, and was feeling pretty chilly along the spine whenever I thought of it. The judge was with the party, and the only way I ever did win that suit was by pretending not to see the chickens hide under the corn-shocks the minute he got off his horse. He'd eat a whole pullet every meal, and he got around so often they all knew him—some by sight and some by hearsay."

He drew the map toward him and indicated a spot by holding the point of his knife on it.

"There's a strip along here," he began, and Griffith arose and bent over the map, "that I can't make out. That seems to be an opening in the mountains; but——"

"No—no," said Griffith, taking up a pencil from the table. "No; the real opening—the road pass—— Let me see; what's the scale of miles here? M-m-m! Four? No— Why, the road pass is at least five miles farther on." He drew a line. "You see, it's like this. There." He stopped and shook his head. "M-m-m! No, n-o-o; that map's all wrong. It ought to run along there—so. This way. The road—the *wagon* road—trends along here—so. Then you go across the ridge at an angle here—so. There ought to be a stream here. O pshaw! this map's— Where did you get this map? It's no account, at all. Why, according to this, there's at least seven miles left out right here, between— Why, right here, where they've got those little, insignificant-looking foothills, is one of the most rugged and impassable places in this world! Here, now!" He drew several lines and turned the map. "O pshaw! there's no place left now for the— Here, right a-b-o-u-t h-e-r-e—no, there, right there—is the Bedolph estate—fine old stone house, corn-fields, wheat, orchards—a splendid place. Then, as you go up this way, you pass into a sort of pocket—a little strip pretty well hedged in. You couldn't go with a carriage without making a circuit around here—this way—but a horseman can cut all that off and go—so. See? There is a mill—fine old mill stream—right here—runs this way."

Mr. Lincoln had followed every line eagerly, making little vocal sounds of understanding, or putting in a single word to lead Griffith on. Suddenly he said:

"You're a good Union man Morton tells me."

"I am, indeed, Mr. Lincoln. Nobody in the world could be more sorry than I over the present situation. I——"

"How sorry are you?"

"What do you mean?" asked Griffith, straightening up. Mr. Lincoln arose at the same time.

"How much of a Union man are you?—

'nough to help save it? How sorry are you?—sorry enough to act?"

Griffith had almost forgotten why he was here. It all came back to him. He began to breathe hard.

"I have acted. I have helped," he said, moving toward the window. "When you came in the room I was looking through those fine glasses of yours at that bridge, across which I came in fifty-three, self-exiled, hastening to escape from the bondage of ownership, and, at the last, from the legal penalty of leaving behind me two freed, runaway negroes." He had lifted the glasses to his eyes again. "I thought then that I had done my full duty—*all* of it. But since then I have given my three sons to you—to my country. They——"

Mr. Lincoln's muscular hand rested on Griffith's shoulder.

"Look at that bridge again. Do you see any dead men on it? Do you see young sons like your own dragging bleeding limbs across it? Do you see terror-stricken horses struggling with and trampling down those wounded boys? Do you see——"

Griffith turned to look at him, in surprise.

"No," he said, "nothing of the kind. There are a few soldiers moving about down this side, but there's nothing of that kind."

He offered the glasses to the President, who waved them away.

"I don't need them!" and an inexpressibly sad expression crossed his face. "I don't need them. I have seen it. I saw it all one day. I saw it all that night as it trailed past here. I heard the groans. The blood was under that window. I have seen it! I have seen nothing else since. If you have never seen a panic of wounded men, pray to your God that you never may!" The sorrowful voice was attuned now to the sorrowful, the tragic face. "Do you see that lounge over there?" He pointed to the other side of the room. "Men think it is a great thing to be a President of a great nation —and so it is, so it is; yet for three nights while you slept peacefully in your bed I lay there, when I wasn't reading telegrams or receiving messages, not knowing what would come next—waiting to be ready for whatever it might be."

He waited for the full effect of his words, but Griffith did not speak.

"I was waiting to be ready for whatever did come," he repeated, slowly, "and to give my whole soul, mind, heart, intellect, and body, if need be, to my country's service. I could not sit back in my arm-chair and say that I have done my share—I had done enough! If I knew how to save or prevent a repetition of that horror, had I done my share—had I done my duty—until I *did* prevent it?"

Griffith began to understand. He sank heavily into a chair, and drew his hand slowly over his forehead again and again. His eyes were closed, but the President was studying the face grimly as he went on: "If a man is drowning, have you done your whole duty if you swim to shore and call back to him that you got out? If——"

"Mr. Lincoln, I——" began Griffith, but the astute man heard still a note of protest in the voice under the note of pain, and he did not allow him to finish.

"If there is but one way to stop all this horrible suffering, this awful carnage, and there is some one who knows how to do it, who is responsible for its continuance? This Union is going to be maintained if there is not a soul left to enjoy its blessings but the widows and orphans the war for its life has made!" he said, bringing his great muscular fist down on the table, and Griffith opened his eyes and sat staring at him with a pain-distorted face. "This war is not for fun! It is not waged for conquest! It is not *our* choice; but the people of this Nation have placed me at the head of this Nation to sustain its integrity—to maintain this Union against all foes, and by the Eternal I am going to do it! You will help us if indeed you are a Union man! You will desert us in our hour of need if you are simply a self-indulgent moralist, who feeds expensive pap to his personal conscience, but gives a stone to his starving neighbor! This Government needs *you*. It needs exactly what you are able to give. Are you its friend or its enemy?"

Griffith had shifted his position uneasily as the torrent of words had poured from the lips of the fire-inspired man before him. Lincoln's long arm had flung out toward him with a gesture of appeal, but he did not wait for a reply. He had not finished presenting the case in light in which he felt sure it would touch the character of the man before him.

"Are your small personal needs paramount to those of your country? Have you no patriotism? Have you no *mercy* upon our soldiers? Must more hundreds of them suffer defeat and death for the lack of what *you* can give them? Are you willing to receive the benefits of a free country which you are not willing to help in her hour of greatest need? Can you—do you—want to leave your young sons and the sons of your neighbors on the far side of the dead line marked by that bridge?" The allusion was a chance one, but it struck home.

Griffith put out his hand.

"What do you want me to do?" he gasped, hoarsely.

The President grasped his hand and held it in a vice-like grip. "What—do—I—want—you—to—do?" he asked, with a deliberation strangely at variance with the passion of his words a moment ago. He looked down searchingly, kindly, pityingly into the troubled eyes before him. "What do I want you to do? I—want — you — to — follow—your—conscience—for—the—benefit—of— your — country — instead — of—for — your— own —personal—comfort,—until—that — conscience — tells — you — your—country—needs—you—no—longer; that you have, in deed and in truth, done your share fully! I want you to go with an advance guard down through that very country"—his long finger pointed to the disfigured map on the table—" and show our commander the *real* topography of that land. I want you to make him as familiar with it as you are yourself. I want you to show him where the passes and fords are, where supplies can be carried across, where water is plenty, and where both advance and retreat are possible without useless and horrible slaughter. I want you—" He was still holding Griffith's right hand. He placed his left on his shoulder again. "No man has done his duty in a crisis like this until he has done *all* that he can to hasten the dawn of peace;" he lowered his voice, "and he that is not with us is against us," he said solemnly, the scriptural language falling from his lips as if their professions were reversed.

"How far do you want me to go?" asked Griffith, looking up with an appeal in every tense muscle of his miserable face. "It is my native State! They are my people! I love every foot of ground—I love those—" He was breathing so hard he stopped for a moment. "That we do not think alike—that they are what you call rebels to our common country—does not change my love. I—Mr. Lincoln——"

The President seemed to tower up to a greater height than even his former gigantic altitude. He threw both arms out in a sudden passion: "Forget your love! Forget your native State! Forget *yourself!* Forget *everything* except that this Union must and shall be saved, and that *you* can hasten the end of this awful carnage!" The storm had swept over. He lowered his voice again, and with both hands on the preacher's shoulders: "I will agree to this. When you have gone so far that you can come back here to me and say, 'I *know* now that I have done enough. My conscience is clear. My whole duty is done.' When you can come back here and say that to me—when you can say (if you and I had changed places) that you could ask no more of me—then I will agree to ask no more of you." Then, suddenly, "When will you start? To-night?"

"Yes," said Griffith, almost inaudibly, and sank into a chair.

Mr. Lincoln strode to the table and pushed aside the disfigured map. "I will write your instructions and make necessary plans," he said. "There is not much to do. The General and the engineer corps are ready. I hoped and believed you would go." His pen flew over the paper. Then he paused and looked at his visitor. "We must fix your rank. Will you volunteer, or shall I——?"

"Is that necessary, Mr. Lincoln? I am a preacher, you know. I—— Can't I go just as I am—just—as——?"

The President had turned again to the table, and was writing. Griffith stepped to his side.

"Do you realize, Mr. Lincoln, that every man, woman and child in that whole country will recognize me—and——?"

"Yes, yes, I know, I know. We must do

everything we can to protect you from all danger—against assassination or——"

"It is not *that*," said Griffith, hoarsely. "Do you care nothing for the good-will—for the confidence—of your old neighbors back in Illinois?"

The stroke went directly home.

"Do I care for it?" There was a long pause. The sunken eyes were drawn to a mere line. "I'd rather lose anything else in this world. It is meat and drink to me. I—— Look here, Mr. Davenport; don't make the mistake of thinking that I don't realize what I'm asking you to do—that I don't see the sacrifice. I do. I do, fully, and I want to do everything I can to—to make it up to you. I know you used to be greatly trusted and beloved down there. Morton has told me. He told me all about the pathos of that old negro following you, too, and how you made out to keep her. I know, I know it all, and I wouldn't ask you if I knew how to avoid it. I tell you that I'd rather give up everything else in this world than the good-will of those old friends of mine back there in Illinois; but if I had to give up the respect and confidence and love of every one of them, or forfeit that of Abraham Lincoln, who has sworn to sustain this Union, I'd have to stick to old Abe! It would go hard with me — harder than anything I know of — but it would have to be done. We have *got* to sustain this Union! We'll save her with slavery at the South and with friends to ourselves, if we can; but, by the Eternal! we'll save her anyhow!"

He struck over and over the same chord—the Union must be saved. Every road led back to that one point. Every argument hinged upon it. Every protest was met by it. He hammered down all other questions.

"If we are Union men, this is the time and the place to show it. All other objects, motives, methods, private interests, tastes, loves or preferences must yield to the supreme test— What are we willing to do to save the Union?"

Once he said:

"You don't suppose my position is particularly agreeable, do you? Do you fancy it is easy, or to my liking?"

"No, no, Mr. President, of course not. I understand that; but you are holding a public office, and——"

"So are you," came like a shot. "In times like this *all* men who are or who have been trusted by their fellow men, are now, in a sense, leaders—are in a public position. Their influence is for or against this Union. There is no neutral ground. I've already been driven a good deal farther than I ever expected to have to go, and it looks as if I'd have to jump several more fences yet; but you'll see me jump 'em when the time comes, or I'll break my neck trying it!" He wheeled back to the table. "Here, why not let me put you down as a chaplain? Carry you on the rolls that way? It——"

"No, Mr. Lincoln, that won't do. I won't agree to that. If I go it is not as chaplain. We know that, and there must be no pretense. I will not use my ministerial standing as a cloak. I——"

"You are right, too. I wouldn't, myself. Then you won't be with any one division long at a time. You'll have to transfer as the need comes. Let me see—m-m-m——"

"If I do this thing I will do it outright. I'll

ask one thing of you—I don't want it known; for, of course, none of my friends can understand the way you look at it and the way you have made me see it. But when I go, I'll want a good horse, and I'll ride in the lead. I'll not stay back as a chaplain, nor sutler, nor as anything but as what I shall be, God help me! a guide!"

"Well, suppose we just call you that—Government Guide. But since it is to be such extraordinary service—so vital to our cause—we'll make your pay extraordinary, too. How does a colonel's pay strike you?"

Griffith was on his feet in a flash. He stood looking straight at the President, who had not turned as he asked the question. The hands of the preacher were grasping the back of his chair.

"On the pay-roll," began Mr. Lincoln, "you will appear as——"

"Pay-roll! Pay-roll!" burst from Griffith, and the President turned. The expression of the preacher's face was a complete surprise, but the astute man understood it instantly. Griffith was moving toward the door. "Mr.

Lincoln, you do not understand me. You have mistaken your man! You—I——"

The President had followed him hastily and his own hand reached the door first.

"Stop!" he said kindly. "It is *you* who do not understand *me*. I——"

"I understood you twice to say—to offer to *pay* me to lead a hostile army—to take troops into—to the homes of——"

"No, no, don't look at it that way. It is right you should have some—some—rank—and——" He was going to utter again the word pay, but did not. Suddenly he thought of a way out of the dilemma.

"You see, it is like this. You've got to have grub—rations. Now, we can't issue rations to men who don't exist—ain't doing some sort of service, don't y' see? Then suppose you should be captured. I don't want to suppose anything of the kind, and of course we've got to take every possible precaution against such a disaster—but suppose you *were* captured, unless you are recognized as—unless you have some status—we can't require the rebels to treat you as a prisoner of war and exchange you for some officer. We've got to arrange so you will be treated as a regular, and an important prisoner of war—don't you see?" The dangerous shoals were being skilfully crossed. The sagacious lawyer and reader of men was retrieving his blunder. He passed his hand through Griffith's arm, and turned him from the door. "*That was what I meant!* We'll have to carry you, somehow, on the rolls—for rations and things. You'll mess with the General, of course, and we'll see that you have the very best horse in the army—you see, I know the circuit rider's weakness. The fact is——" He was leading Griffith back to the table where the great disfigured map lay—where he deftly slipped the paper containing the half-written instructions, upon which the subject of pay had been begun, under its edge, took another sheet in its stead, and began anew with the rank and the pay left out.

CHAPTER XVI.

"Into the valley of death."—*Tennyson.*

It was arranged that the command with which Griffith moved should, so far as was possible, avoid collision with the enemy; move silently, swiftly or slowly as occasion demanded, but at all times do everything possible to give to the topographical engineers a clear, distinct and minute knowledge of the country, so that in future intelligent action could be sustained. It was thought wise to take as few troops as safety would permit, and, wherever knowledge of the proximity of the Southern forces was obtained in time, take some other road or retire temporarily to the seclusion of the mountains. All fighting was, if possible, to be avoided. This was the plan of operations. At times they were far inside the enemy's lines, but at distant points from the opposing force.

At other times they were again camped for a night with some advance division of the federal troops farther northward. To those to whom their object was unknown, their movements would have seemed unaccountable, indeed.

In road or pass or village, many a familiar face did Griffith see, and his relief was intense, if no look of recognition came into it. His fatigue coat, from which the brass buttons had been taken, and broad-brimmed, cord-decorated military hat, served as something of a disguise with those who had never seen him in other than clerical garb. Often a sharp pain shot through his heart as he rode through some one of his old circuits, and a one time friendly face looked up at him, at first with simply the curiosity and dislike bestowed upon the staff officers of a hostile force, and then with a sudden flash of recognition, there would come, also, a look of bitter personal resentment, not meant for the staff, but for that son of the South, who, as they felt, was betraying his friends. What his position or rank was they did not know. His uniform was that of a civilian, excepting only the hat; but that he was in and with and of the invading army was enough. The information spread like wildfire.

"Griffith Davenport is with a brigade of Yankees! He knows every inch of this country!" What this meant to both sides, was quickly understood. Bitterness increased. That he should be shot at the first opportunity was universally conceded. Griffith saw and felt it keenly. It made his heart too heavy for words. At first he spoke to the General: "I knew that man, General. He recognized me. Did you see how he turned suddenly to look again? Did you see——?"

"Yes, I noticed, and I saw the look of hate, damn him; but you needn't be afraid. The first time any assassination business is tried they will find who they have got to deal with. I'll burn every God-damned house I come to, and shoot several citizens in retaliation! Oh, I'm not half so mild as I look! Don't you be afraid! They'll all think hell has broke loose on earth, if they fire from ambush at you! They'll have to get you in open battle, if they want to be treated with soldierly consideration, and we don't intend you to be in any battle ; so don't you be——"

"It is not that! It is not that, General," Griffith would say. He tried to explain.

"Well, heavens and earth! What did you expect? You didn't expect 'em to *like* it, did you?"

Griffith sighed and gave it up. No, he did not expect them to like it. He did not even hope that they could understand it fairly, and yet—— The home-coming was indeed bitter, and Griffith ceased to sing. He saw maps made of the places he loved, and he saw in the distance the peaceful old haunts filled with contending armies. He looked at the trees that were still old and warm and loyal friends, in spite of difference of creed or politics, and he dreamed of them when they should be lopped of their branches and torn with shot and shell as they tried vainly to shield with their own sturdy limbs those who knew no better than to fight the battles of this life with sword and gun. One day, as he rode slowly in advance of the rest, he suddenly looked up toward the gnarled branch of a great tree, where he recalled that an old friend of his had lived. The heads of three tiny squirrels peeped out, and the mother frisked hard by. "Ah," he said, aloud, "how do you do, Bunnie? Still living at the old home-place, I see! Is it you or your great-grandchildren? There's such a strong family likeness I can't tell." The little animal whisked nearer, and looked with curious eyes that were not afraid. "You do not blame me, and you do not hate me, and you do not fear me, Bunnie. You understand me better than men do, after all." He sighed and tossed a bit of cracker toward the nest. It fell far short, but the mother-squirrel whisked about here and there, and flipped her tail and posed; but at last snatched up the proffered gift and scampered up the tree. Griffith smiled.

"I've broken bread with one of my old friends at last," he said aloud.

"What did you say?" asked the General, halting suddenly. He had lowered his voice to the danger pitch, as he had mistaken Griffith's low tone for one of caution. He lifted his hand, and each of his officers down the line did the same. There was an instant halt.

"What was it?" he asked again, under his breath.

"A nest of squirrels right where they were fifteen or twenty years ago. I was renewing the acquaintance. *They* were the first old friends that have not been afraid of—who trusted me still. I was——"

A volley of oaths burst forth. "Attention! March!" he commanded, and as the line officers repeated the command, the General's wrath waxed furious. He did not dare to wreak it directly upon Griffith. He dashed back down the line, swearing with that lurid facility and abandon for which he was famous, at the astonished, but case-hardened and amused men.

"Halted an army to talk to a God-damned squirrel!" he ground out between his wrathful teeth, as he rejoined his staff. He whipped out a revolver and fired at the nest. The bullet flew wide of the mark, but the little heads disappeared in affright. The staff-officers looked at each other and smiled. The contrast between the two at their head was a source of constant, mild fun.

"Broken faith with even you, haven't I, Bunnie?" said Griffith, softly, as he rode on. "Do you think I threw you the cracker so that I could the better shoot you? I didn't, Bunnie,—but you will never know."

A half-mile further on Griffith halted. "General," he said, "this is the only place for some distance now that we can halt for the night under cover of a dense wood and still have water near. There is a creek just below that rise. It is good water. It curves around this way, and the horses can be picketed near it and still be hid. After this it will be open country for ten miles or more. If——"

"Halt! Throw out pickets! Dismount! Break ranks!"

The orders were given and repeated. The appearance of a camp grew up like magic. No fires were to be lighted until scout and picket reports came in, but the men went about feeding their horses and making ready for the fires and for "grub," as they called it. They were glad to stretch themselves. It had been a long day's ride.

"We will signal from the rise over there, General," Griffith said, "If from there we can see no camp-fires, there will be none near enough to detect ours. Shall I return here, General, or——"

"Return here. Pick your escort."

Griffith rode away with his three sharpshooters. The tired men watched eagerly for the signal, as they lay about on the ground. A shout went up when they saw it, and fires were lighted and rations brought forth. A young fellow with corporal's straps was humming as he lay on his back with both feet far up on the body of a tree. He had carried with him all day an empty tin can, and now he was making coffee in it. He turned from time to time to peer into the can or readjust the sticks as they burned.

"We're tenting to-night on the old camp-ground."

His soft tenor rang out on the cool evening air as clear as the note of a bird, despite his recumbent position. He lifted himself on one elbow and peered again into the coffee, but the song ran on—

"Give us a song to cheer."

A group near him was deep in a game of cards. "Here! It's Towsy's deal! Damned if I don't believe Jim would deal every hand if he wasn't watched. He——"

"Our weary heart, a song of home——"

"Oh, dry up! Give us a rest!"

"Ouch! Stop that! If I don't——"

"Clubs again, by gad! Every time Stumpy deals, its clubs. I believe——"

"And friends we love so dear.
Many are the hearts that are weary to-night,
Wishing——"

The clear tenor had risen into steady continuity as the young corporal sat half up to shake the tin can again. The card dealer joined in with a mocking bass, then suddenly, voice after voice took up the refrain and the very air seemed to come laden with it, from far and near. The volume of sound died with the last note of the refrain, and once more the clear tenor, lying on his back now, with both hands under his head, ran softly on alone:

'We've been tenting to-night on the old camp-ground,
Thinking of days gone by——"

He drew a letter from his breast-pocket, and, as he unfolded it, stooped over and took one swallow of the coffee, and replaced the can on the fire. Some hard tack lay beside him, and one biscuit reposed on his stomach where he replaced it when he lay back again, and finished the verse slowly. When the refrain began again, the cards were held down, men in other groups straightened up from rekindling fires, others stopped short in a game of quoits played with horseshoes picked up on the banks of the creek. Water carriers set down their loads, or halted, with pails still in hand, and added their voices to the melody. The effect amongst the trees was indescribable. The picket in the distance half halted in his tramp, and turned to listen. The moon was beginning to swing up over the hill, from which the signal had come, and between the trees it touched the face of the delicate-featured young corporal of the sweet voice, and he turned the letter to catch the light from it, and add to the glow of the firelight, that he might the better re-read the treasured words. He was still humming softly, inarticulately, now. A stick burned in two, and the can of precious coffee was slowly emptying its overturned contents on the ground.

There was but one bite gone from the biscuit which lay on the blue coat. Music and sentiment had triumphed over appetite and the young corporal dozed off, asleep now with the letter still in his hand and the noisy players about him. In the distance Griffith and his escort were returning. Suddenly a shot rang out in the clear air! Then another and another! The men were on their feet in an instant. The General was hastily adjusting his field-glass, but in the moonlight it was but slight help. He could see, as the smoke cleared away, six men instead of four. So much he could make out, but no more. One was being lifted on to a horse. All were dismounted. There was activity in the camp. Hasty preparations were made to send a relief party. Who was shot? What did it mean? Was there an ambush? Was the Guide deceived as to the safety of this position? Would they have to fight or retreat? Had the Guide been killed? Had some angry native seen and assassinated Griffith? The officers consulted together hastily and orders were given, but the little procession was slowly approaching.

They were not pursued. At least there was not to be a battle—and there had been a capture, but who was killed? The Government Guide? Two were walking—were they the assassin and his companion? When the little procession reached the picket line it halted and there was some readjustment of the body they were carrying, stretched between two horses, where it lay motionless except as others lifted it. Beside it walked another figure not in the federal uniform. Tall, lank, grim, and limping painfully, with a blood-stain on the shoulder and a bullet hole in the hat. The sharp-shooters had done their work—but who was it —*what* was it that lay across those two horses that they were leading? The whole camp was watching and alert. Cards, quoits, letters had disappeared. At last they could see that the Body was not Griffith. He still sat astride his splendid chestnut horse and the relief party were talking to him. The procession moved to the General's tent. Griffith looked pale and troubled. The sharpshooters were radiant. The Body was lifted down, and its long pendant beard was matted and massed with blood,

The pride, the joy, the ambition of Whiskers Biggs was brought low at last! He was breathing still, but the feeble hand essayed in vain to stroke the voluminous ornament and ambition of his life. The hand hung limp and mangled by his side. The General questioned the other prisoner in vain. He pointed to Griffith and preserved an unbroken silence. Griffith spoke to him aside. The prisoner turned slowly to the commander:

"I'll tell *him*. Few words comprehend th' whole." Then he lapsed into silence again and nothing could induce him to speak. The General threatened, coaxed and commanded in vain. The imperturbable mountaineer stood like one who heard not. All that the sharpshooters could tell was soon told. Some one had fired from ambush, apparently at Griffith. They had returned the fire instantly. Then they had found this man who was dying and the other one beside him. "I know this man, General," said Griffith. "He says that he will talk to me alone. May I—shall I——"

"He'll talk to *me*, God damn him! or he'll get a dose of—— Did you fire at our men?"

he demanded of the mountaineer. Lengthy Patterson shifted his position to relieve his wounded leg. He gazed stolidly, steadily, expressionlessly before him, and uttered not a sound. His gun had been taken from him, and his hands seemed worse than useless without this his one and only companion from whom he never separated. The hands moved about in aimless action like the claws of some great lobster.

"It will go a good deal easier with you, you infernal idiot, if you'll out with your story— tell your side of it. How'd this thing happen?"

Lengthy glanced sidewise at the Body as it lay on the ground. "Friend of mine," he said, and lapsed into silence again.

"Will you tell me, Lengthy?" asked Griffith. "Will you tell me in the presence of the General? It would be better for us both if you will. I wish——"

"'Twill?" asked Lengthy giving Griffith a long, slow look. "Better fer yoh?"

"Yes," said Griffith, half choking up. He thought he had solved the problem of why, with these two mountaineer marksmen as their antagonists none of their party had been shot in the encounter. "Yes, better for me. Do you care for that, Lengthy?" The woodsman gave another long look at Griffith, and then pointed with his thumb at the figure on the ground.

"I done hit. Whis aimed t' kill yoh. Few words comp——" Griffith grasped the great rough, helplessly groping hands in his. "I thought so, I thought so," he said brokenly. "And you stood by me even——" He was your friend, and——" Griffith's voice broke. In the pause that followed Lengthy was staring at the form on the ground.

"Yes. Whis wus a frien' er mine; but Whis tuck aim at yoh. Few-words-comprehends-th'-whole!" The last sentence seemed to be all one word. Griffith was still holding the great hands.

"Did you know I was with Northern troops, Lengthy? Did you know——?"

"Knowed hit wus you. Didn't keer who t'other fellers wus. He tuck aim. Seed whar he wus pintin'—Few words——"

"Are you a Union man, Lengthy?"

"Naw."

"Rebel, are you?" asked the General, sharply. There was a profound silence. The mountaineer did not even turn his head.

"I asked you if you were a rebel. God damn you! Can't you hear?" shouted the General thoroughly angry. "I'll let you know——"

"Are you on the Confederate side, Lengthy?" began Griffith. The mountaineer had not indicated in any way whatever that he had heard any previous question. "Naw," he said slowly and as if with a mental reservation. The General shot forth a perfect volley of oaths and questions and threats, but the immobility of the mountaineer remained wholly undisturbed. There was not even the shadow of a change of expression on the bronzed face.

"What the General wants to know—what *I* want to know is, Lengthy, which side are you on? Are you——"

"On yourn."

"On Davenport's side against the world!" remarked a staff officer aside, smiling. The mountaineer heard. He turned slowly until the angle of his vision took in the speaker.

"On his side agin the worl'. Few words——"

The rest was drowned in a shout of laughter, in which the irascible Commander joined. Griffith's eyes filled. Lengthy saw—and misinterpreted. He forgot the wound in his leg, and that his trusty gun was his no more. He sprang to Griffith's side.

"On his side agin the *hull* o' yuh!" he said, like a tiger at bay. The sorely tried leg gave way and he fell in a heap at Griffith's feet.

"Here! Quick! Get the surgeon. We forgot his wounds. He is shot in the leg and here——" Griffith was easing the poor fellow down as he talked, trying to get him into a better position. Some one offered him a canteen. The surgeon came and began cutting the boot from the swollen leg.

"Do *everything* for him, Doctor—everything you would for me," said Griffith hoarsely. "He killed his friend and risked his own life to save me. He——"

His voice broke and he walked away into the darkness. Presently Lengthy opened his eyes and asked feebly, "Whar's the Parson?"

"Who?"

"Th' Parson."

"Oh," said the surgeon kindly, "you want the Chaplain. Oh, you're not going to die! You're all right! You've lost a lot of blood and stood on that leg too long, but——"

"Whah's Parson Dav'npoht?"

A light dawned upon the surgeon. He had never thought of Griffith as a clergyman only as he had heard it laughed over that the General swore so continuously in his presence. He sent for Griffith. When he came Lengthy saw that his eyes were red. He motioned the others to go away. Then he whispered, "Th' other fellers —our soldiers—th'——"

"You mean the Confederate troops, the Southern men?" asked Griffith, and Lengthy nodded; "Jest over yander. Layin' fer ye."

"I looked everywhere for smoke, Lengthy. I didn't see any signs of camp fires. I——"

"Jest what me an' Whis was doin' fer t'other side when we seed ye. Hain't got no fires. Hain't goin' t' make none."

"Do you mean that you were doing a sort of scout or advance duty for the reb—the Confederates, when you met us, Lengthy?"

He nodded. "Jest thet."

"You were to go back and tell them about——"

"We wus. Saw you. Didn't go. Him 'n' me qua'l'd 'bout——"

"About shooting me?"

Lengthy nodded again. "He aimed at ye. I got him fust." There was a long pause.

"Do you want to go back to your camp, Lengthy, if——"

"Naw."

Presently he said: "They's mo' o' them then they is o' you alls."

Griffith grasped his idea. "You think we better leave here? You think they will attack?"

"Kin leave me layin' here. They'll git me—'n' *him*;" he pointed with his thumb again toward the friend of his life—the body that lay awaiting burial on the morrow.

"Would you rather go with us?" began Griffith, and the swarthy face lightened up.

"Kin you alls take me?"

"Certainly, certainly, if you want to go. We won't leave you. The General——"

"Hain't goin' with him. Goin' 'th you."

"All right, all right, Lengthy. You shall go

with *me* and you shall *stay* with me." The mountaineer turned his head slowly. The narcotic the surgeon had given was overcoming him. He did not understand it, and he was vainly struggling against a sleep which he did not comprehend.

"You—alls—better—light—out. They is mo' o' them and—they—is mad—plum—through. Few—words—com—com——"

The unaccustomed effort at linguistic elaboration exhausted him, and, together with the sleeping potion, Lengthy was rendered unconscious of all pain, and an hour later he was borne on a stretcher between two horses as the engineers' party silently retraced its steps and left the camp deserted and desolate with its one silent occupant lying stark in the moonlight, with its great mass of matted beard upon its lifeless breast.

CHAPTER XVII.

"At first happy news came, in gay letters moiled
With my kisses,—of camp life and glory."
Browning.

THE fall and winter wore on. Spring was near. Griffith wrote to Katherine daily and mailed his letters whenever and wherever it was possible. His personal reports of progress went with regularity to Mr. Lincoln, and an occasional note of congratulation or thanks or encouragement came to him in reply. Meantime the Army of the Potomac did little but wait, and the armies of the South and West were active. Letters from the boys came to Katherine with irregular regularity. Those from Howard were always brief and full of an irresponsible gurgle of fun and heroics. He had been in two or three small fights, and wrote of them as if he had enjoyed an outing on a pleasure excursion. He said in one that when he was on picket duty he had "swapped lies and grub" with the picket on the other side. "He tried to stuff me with a lot of fiction about the strength of their force —said they had not less than ninety thousand men in front of us ready to lick us in the morning. I told him that I'd just happened by accident to hear our roll called, and it took two days and a night to read the names of our officers alone. He was a crack liar but I reckon we got off about even. He had the worst old gun I ever saw. It came out of the ark. He admired mine, and it was a tip-top Enfield, but I told him it was just an old borrowed thing (the last of which was true) and that my own was nearly as big as fifty of it and would shoot ten miles. He kicked at me and laughed, but I didn't tell him I was a gunner in a battery. A battery is a jim-dandy of a place. I get to ride all the time. That suits me right down to the ground. I haven't had a scratch yet and I'm not afraid I'll get one." His letters rattled on in some such fashion whenever he remembered or exerted himself enough to write at all. They developed in slang as the months went by, and Katherine smiled and sighed.

Beverly's letters kept up their old tone, and

he tried in every way he could think of, to cheer his mother. He had wholly recovered, he said, from his wounds, and was now with Grant in Tennessee. He described the long moss on the trees, and wrote: "We are moving now toward Corinth. That is the objective point. I was transferred a month ago to Grant's army, and so, unless Roy has been transferred since you wrote me last, I'll get to see him in a few days, I hope. That will be good. It seems as if we boys had traveled a pretty long road in the matter of age and experience since we were at home together. I'm glad to hear of Roy's promotion—the handsome fellow! And so it was for conspicuous bravery at Fort Donaldson, was it? Good! Good! Ah, we can be proud of Roy, mother. And he got only a little flesh-wound in it all, and did not have to go to the hospital at all! What lucky dogs we boys are, to be sure. I hope father is home with you by this time. Of course, I understand the ominous silence and inaction in Virginia—in the army of the Potomac—as only a few of us can. But I do hope that father will do all the President asked of him, and get home before they undertake to act upon the information he is enabling them to gather. Yes, yes, mother, I know how terribly hard he took it, and how silently heroic he is and will be, God bless him! But after all, mother mine, *your* part is about the hardest of all to bear. I think of that more and more! To sit and wait! To silently sit and wait for you know not what. To take no active part! Oh, the heroic patience and endurance that must take! But don't worry about us. The fact is that we are not in half so much danger as you think. When one comes to know how few, after all, of the millions of rounds of ammunition that are fired, ever find their mark in human flesh, one can face them pretty courageously. We were talking it over in camp the other day— a lot of the officers. I really had had no idea what a safe place a battle-field is. It seems that out of 7260 balls fired, only ten hit anybody, and only one of those are serious or fatal! Just look at the chances a fellow has. Why he doesn't seem to be in much more danger than he is that a brick will fall on him as he walks the streets, or that he'll slip and break his neck on the ice. Doesn't seem so very dangerous, now, does it, mother? Now, I want you to remember those figures, for they are correct. Then you remember that I got my three—which is more than my share of balls, in the very first fight I was in; so you see *I'm* not likely to get any more. Roy had one, so his chance to catch any more is poor; and as for Howard—well, somehow or other, I never feel the least anxiety about Howard. He'd pull through a knot-hole if the knot was still in it. He is so irresistibly, irresponsibly, recklessly indifferent. But at all events, mother, don't worry too much. My only anxiety, now, is to hear that father is at home again; both for your sake and for his. Ye gods! what a terrific sacrifice the President demanded of him! And what a stubborn heroism it has taken to make father do it,—with his temperament and feelings,—a heroism and patriotism beyond even the comprehension of most men. Give little Margaret the enclosed note, please. I don't know that she can read it, but I wrote it as plain as I could on this shingle. We are moving pretty steadily now. We stopped to-day, to let the supplies catch up. We start again in an hour or so. We are all ready now.

I never cease to be glad that you have old aunt
Judy, and that she continues such a comfort,
—and trial. Give her my love, and tell the gentle
and buxom Rosanna, that if she were in this
part of the country she'd 'see the loikes av
me' at every turn. Soldiers are thicker than
peas in a pod, and she'd not have 'to go fur t'
foind the loikes av me' multiplied by ten thousand, all of whom 'become their soger close'
quite as truly as did the undersigned when the
admiration of Rosanna for me blossomed forth in
such eloquence and elaboration of diction. This
seems rather a frivolous letter; but I want you
to keep up good heart, little mother. It won't—
it can't—last much longer, and just as soon as
father gets home. I, for one, shall feel quite easy
again. I hope he is there by this time, with his
part all done. The last letter I got from him,
he thought it would not take much longer to
do all they expected him to do, now. Dear
old father! His last letter to me was an inspiration and a sermon, in living (as he is),
without the least bit of preaching in it. He
doesn't need to preach. He lives far better
than any creed or than any religion; but——"

Katherine broke off and pondered. Was Beverly still reading Thomas Paine? If he were to be killed! What did he believe? "Lives far better than any creed or than any religion," what did he mean? Had Beverly become openly an unbeliever in creeds and religions? The thought almost froze her blood. She fell upon her knees and wept and prayed—not for her son's life to be spared from the bullets of the enemy, as was her habit, but that the "shafts of the destroyer" might spare his soul! Her cup of anxiety and sorrow was embittered and made to overflow by the sincerity of a belief which was so simple, and knew so little of evasion, that the bottomless pit did, indeed, yawn before her for this son of her youth.

"Save him! save him!" she moaned aloud, "if not from death, at least from destruction, oh, God of my salvation!"

The terrors which should follow unbelief had been long ago, in her rigid Presbyterian home, made so much a part of her very nature, that the simple, cheerful, happy side of Griffith's religion, which had been uppermost all these years, had not even yet, in cases of unusual stress, obliterated the horror of Katherine's literal belief in and fear of an awful hell, and a vengeance-visiting God for those who slighted or questioned the justice or truth of a cruel revelation of Him. A great and haunting fear for Beverly's soul eclipsed her fear for his life, and Katherine's religion added terrors to the war that were more real and dark and fearful than the real horrors that are a natural and legitimate part of a cruel, civil contest. The "comforts," to a loving heart and a clear head, of such a religion, were vague and shadowy; indeed. Its certain and awful threats were like a flaming sword of wrath ever before her eyes. To those who could evade the personal application of the tenets of their faith, who could accept or reject at will the doctrines they professed, who could wear as an easy garment the parts they liked, and slip from their shoulders the features of their " revelation " to which the condition of their own loved ones did not respond, there might be comfort. But to Katherine there was none. Her faith was so real and firm, that it did not doubt a literal damnation, nor could she read from under the decree those she loved, simply because she loved them. An eternal decree of suffering hung over her first-born, the idol of her soul! The awful burden of her religion was almost more than she could bear in these days of fear and loneliness, stimulated as it was by the ever-present threat and shadow of death for the lamb that had strayed, even so little, from the orthodox fold. Her days were doubly burdened by the new anxiety, shadowed by the real, and haunted by the agony of fear for the imaginary, danger to her son. In her dreams, that night, she saw him stand before an angry and avenging God, and she awoke in a very panic of delirium and mental anguish. Great beads of moisture stood upon her brow. "Save him! save him! oh, God of our salvation!" she cried out, and little Margaret stirred uneasily in her bed.

"Wat dat, honey? Wat dat yoh say, Mis' Kate!" called out Judy from her cot in the next room. "Did yoh call me, Mis' Kate?"

"No, no, aunt Judy, I had a bad dream. I——"

The old woman hobbled in. "Now, des look

aheah, honey, des yoh stop that kine er dreams, now. Dey ain't no uste t' nobody, an' dey des makes bad wuk all de way 'roun'. An' 'sides dat dey ain't got no sense to 'em, nohow." Poor old aunt Judy, her philosophy was deeper and truer than she knew or than her mistress suspected; but the sound of her kind old voice comforted Katherine as no philosophy could.

"Dar now, honey, yoh des lay right down dar 'n' go to sleep agin. Yoah ole aunt Judy des gwine ter stay right heah twell yoah skeer gits gone. Dar now, dar now, honey, dem kine er dreams is all foolishness. Dey is dat! Now, I gwine ter set heah an' yoh des whorl in an' dream sompin' good 'bout Mos Grif, dat's what you do! Aunt Judy gwine ter set right heah by de bed. Dar now, honey! Dar now, go sleep."

CHAPTER XVIII.

"Into the jaws of death,
Into the mouth of hell."

Tennyson.

It had rained in torrents. The stiff clay of the muddy roads was ankle deep. Roy's regiment in camp near the Tennessee river was whiling away its time as best it could. It was generally understood that they were to be joined in a day or two by reinforcements, and then march on to Corinth. Roy knew that Beverly was to be with the expected command. The young lieutenant—a first lieutenant now—was proud and eager. He thought it would be a fine thing for him and Beverly to fight side by side. He meant to show Beverly that he was no longer a boy. A soft silken mustache had come to accent his fresh complexion, and he was as handsome and tall and graceful and erect as a young soldier need be. He carried himself with peculiar grace, and he was an inch taller than Beverly, now. He hoped that he would be taller than his brother, and he walked very erect, indeed, as he thought about it. Then he smiled to himself and said half aloud, "He will be here to-morrow, and I shall give him a great welcome—and a surprise." This was his last thought as he turned on his side, and fell into a soldier's dreamless sleep, in spite of rain and mud, in spite of noise and confusion, in spite of danger and anxiety.

It was the night of the fifth of April. Roy had planned to appear very splendid to his brother on the morrow. He had shaved freshly and brushed his uniform, and rubbed up his new shoulder straps. His sword was burnished, and the boy had smiled to himself many times as he worked over these details, to think how vain he was, and how anxious that Beverly should look pleased and proud when he should see him at his best. He seemed to have slept only a little while when there straggled into his consciousness the sound of a shot, then another and another; then a sudden indescribable noise and confusion roused him wholly. He sprang to his feet.

The gray of the dawning day was here. Bugles were sounding. Confusion, noise, action was on all sides. The camp had been surprised! The enemy was upon them! Grape, canister and Enfield balls tore through the tents. Shells burst; the first vision that met his eyes as he rushed forth, was a horse of one of their own batteries, struggling, moaning, whinnying pitifully with both fore-legs torn away, and the cannon half overturned. An onrushing force of Confederates shouting in triumph. As his own regiment tried to form in line, three terrified horses tore past dragging their fellow, and what was left of the dismantled cannon. They were wounding each other cruelly in their mad frenzy of pain and fright. They fell in one mass of struggling, suffering, panic-stricken flesh into the river and drowned, with their harness binding them together, and to the wreck of their dismantled burden. Everything was confusion. Each regiment was doing its best to form and repulse the terrible onslaught. The surprise had been complete. The scouts had been surrounded and captured, and the pickets killed or driven in at the first charge which had awakened the sleeping camp. The horrors, the disasters and the triumphs of Shiloh had begun!

There was no time to think. Action, alone, was possible—the intuitive action of the soldier. The men formed as best they could, and fought as they fell back, or as they advanced a step, with dogged determination to retrieve lost ground. Some were driven into the river, and when wounded, fell beneath its waves to rise no more. The intrepid Confederates followed up their first dash with persistent determination, in spite of the forced march which had preceded the surprise, and in spite of hunger and uncertainty when their supplies might come. They aimed at nothing short of capture. Then supplies would be theirs without delay. But every foot of ground was being stubbornly contested. Now a gain was made, now a loss. Both sides were fighting with that desperation which makes certain only one thing as the issue of the battle—the certainty of an awful carnage. At such a time it does not seem possible, and yet it is true, that a sense of reckless humor finds place and material to feed its fancy. A good-natured badinage held possession of many of the men.

Roy's regiment had been driven back by the first sudden onrush. It had formed and fought as it went, but it had undoubtedly been forced from its position of advantage on the rise of the hill. They were struggling desperately to regain it. Every man seemed determined to stand again where he had stood an hour before or die in the attempt. A large piece of paper pinned to a tree with a bayonet, attracted Roy's attention as the smoke was lifted for a moment, while they pushed forward inch by inch. The boys had seen its like before. They understood and it acted like a stimulant upon them. Some of the boys laughed outright. The smoke hid the paper. The next volley had driven the Confederates a step farther back. The ground was strewn with their men, lying side by side with those who had fallen from the Northern ranks at the first dash of the enemy. The tree with the paper was a trifle nearer.

"Charge for that challenge, boys! Charge!" shouted Roy, and they responded with a yell and a murderous volley as they ran. It was almost within reach now, but the men who had posted it fought like tigers to hold their ground.

"We'll get it, boys! We'll get it!" rang out with the roar of the battle. At last the tree was only a few feet away. A private dashed out of the line, and grasped the bayonet that held the coveted paper and swung it aloft. The challenge was captured! Even the boys who lay on the ground joined in the triumphal shout and one of them volunteered to reply. He had a good arm left! He took a pencil from his breast pocket, and turned his body painfully, slowly, so that he could write. The stock of his gun was desk enough. He read the captured paper and laughed. "The —— La. presents its compliments to the —— Ind., and intends to thrash it out of its boots—as usual."

The wounded man turned the paper over and wrote: "The —— Ind. returns its compliments to the —— La. and expresses a desire to see it accomplish the job." He was so near to the tree that he thought he could drag himself to it and post up the reply on the far side, but his legs were numb and helpless, and the pain of dragging himself on hands and hips conquered him. He looked all about him. The ambulance workers had come, not far away, to carry off the wounded. One came near and offered to help him.

"Pin that paper to the far side of that tree, first," he said, with a grim smile. "I'll wait."

The man refused, but the wounded fellow essaying to drag himself toward it again, he yielded, and the return challenge was posted. Two hours later its work was done. The —— La. held the hill again! A laughing shout went up. It might have been a warmly contested game of football, so free from malice was it.

All over the great battle-field the work of the day was back and forth over the same bloody and trampled ground. The mud of the morning took on another tinge of red, and the mingled blood of the gallant fellows who gave their lives for the side they had espoused made hideous mortar of the ghastly sacrifice. The river ran on its way to the sea, floating the costliest driftwood ever cast by man as an offering to his own passions, mistakes, and ambitions; a driftwood pale and ghastly, clad in gray or in blue, and scattering from Maine to Texas, from ocean to ocean, the sorrow that travels in the wake of war, the anguish of those who silently wait by the fireside, for the step that will never come, for the voice that is silent forever! Ah, the ghastliness of war! Ah, the costliness of war! It is those who do not fight who pay the heaviest debt and find its glory ashes!

On the hill was the rivalry of the challenge. It gave grim humor to the contest. Three challenges were taken, and three replaced, before the sunset brought that suspension of effort which left the hill, the tree, and the final glory of the day in the hands of the Confederates. The drawn battle was over for the night, but the trend of the victory was southward, and the heavens once more deluged the dead and dying with the pitiless downpour of chilling rain all the night long. In the northern camp the tired men slept in spite of rain and mud and distant cannonading. With the slain beside them, the groans of the dying about them, the echo of the conflict in their ears, the promise of the struggle of the morrow, still the tired men slept! In the Confederate camp sleep was impossible. The Federal relief boats had come! To-morrow fresh men would fill the Northern ranks. Meantime the thunder of the great gunboats continued the unequal contest. Shot and shell fell with the rain into the Confederate camp. All night the bombardment went on. The river was tinged with red, the heavens kept up the old refrain and wept for the sins, the mistakes, the cruelties of men, and still the tired soldiers slept and waited for the morrow—and what? There would be no more surprises at least. Both understood now that it was a stubborn fight. Both knew that the reinforcements were here for the Federal troops. Pickets and scouts were wide awake now: no danger of another surprise. All night the relief corps worked. All night the distant echoes from the gunboats brought hope to the one and desperation to the other army. All night the surgeons labored. All night stragglers came in dragging wounded limbs. All night suffering horses neighed and whinnied and struggled and at last died from loss of blood —and still men slept! Ah, the blessed oblivion and relief of sleep! If to-morrow's action must come, then to-night nature must restore the wasted energy, and repair the deathly exhaustion,—and men slept! Soaked through with rain, begrimed with smoke and with mud, assailed with groans and with that insidious foe of rest, uncertainty, still men slept, soundly, profoundly, dreamlessly!

The first gray streak of dawn brought a bugle call; another, another. The clouds were clearing away. Nature was preparing to witness another and more desperate struggle. The dreamless sleep, that had refused to yield to hunger, pain, uproar or anxiety, yielded at the first note of the réveille. Every man was awake, alert, active. The rain and action-stiffened limbs were ready for duty again. The seventh of April had dawned. Reinforcements would soon land; but the battle was on before they could disembark. The Confederates, flushed with the advantage of the day before, were determined to overwhelm even the new force. The battle was on. Roy, the spruce, trim, handsome young lieutenant of the day before, waiting for his brother with proud, brotherly anxiety, was a sorry sight to-day, but that did not trouble him. His new shoulder-straps were tarnished, his sword was marked with an ugly red stain, his freshly brushed uniform was bespattered and wrinkled and wet, mud-covered and torn; but he was unhurt save for the track of a Minie ball under the skin of his left arm. To that he gave no heed. A plaster of the pottery clay, self-applied, had taken the soreness almost away, and as Roy stood at the head of his company to-day and took the place of the captain, who would respond to roll-call no more, he was wondering if Beverly would be with the troops that would land, and if they would help save the day. He hoped that Beverly would be there, and yet—after the sights and experiences of yesterday—*did* he hope that Beverly would be there? Beverly might be killed! He had not thought of that the day before, nor had it troubled him for himself; but as he looked about him now or bent to see if an old comrade were really dead, or only unconscious, he somehow felt glad that Beverly had not been there the day before. Ah, these hearts of ours!—these hearts of ours! What tricks they play us! What cowards they make of us! What selfishness they breed in us! For ourselves we can be brave, defiant, even jocose, in the midst of danger or of sorrow; but for those we love! Ah, for those we love, our philosophy is scant comfort, our courage is undermined before it is tested, and we are helpless in the face of Love. We can walk bravely enough into the mouth of a cannon, but Love disarms us, and we cry for mercy where we did not shrink from death!

Roy wondered how much Beverly knew of the battle, and if his heart was anxious, also. He knew Beverly's division was expected, but he thought as he fought, " I reckon I'd just as lieve Beverly shouldn't be with them. If he were on sick leave or—or—something." He felt a little sense of shame for the thought, and fought the more determinedly because of it. The gallant Confederates were flushed by their gain of the day before. No one would have dreamed that they were exhausted by a long march before the surprise. No one would have dreamed that they were hungry, and that their supply-wagons had not come up until long after the struggle. No one would have dreamed that they had been kept up all night by the bombardment from the distant gunboats. No one would have dreamed that out of that intrepid —— Louisiana, with its challenge again on the tree there, would never muster again over three hundred and twenty-seven of the six hundred merry fellows who flung themselves up that hill only twelve short hours ago!

"Our side bet is up, boys, by the jumping jingo!" said one of the relieved pickets the first thing in the morning. "It is written on a slab this time. I don't know when they got it up. I laid for it all night, and was going to pick the fellow off who came out to that tree, but it was darker than a pile of coke last night, and, if hell ever saw such a rain before, the fires must all be out—soaked through. Don't believe there is a dry spot in the devil's domain to-day. Whew! Look at my boots! I had to stop and scrape the mud off every four steps all night long. My feet were as big as a horse's head—and it's mighty good Bible mud, too—sticketh closer than a brother."

The boys had laughed and agreed that they would get the new challenge somehow. The news that it was up again, and on a substantial slab, which seemed to aggravate the offense in some inexplicable way, spread and aroused the young fellows anew. They would have that slab or die in the attempt. The side bet, as they called it, must be won. They were making straight for it, and the Confederates were holding their position with grim and dogged determination. A sudden onrush of fresh, eager, rested, enthusiastic men, yelling as they came from the gunboats, dashed from the steamboat landing and flung themselves against the lines. The relief had come! Regiment after regiment dashed past. Every new one was felt like a blast of cold wind in the face of a belated traveler. The Confederate lines wavered, broke, rallied, retreated, reformed. More fresh troops came and swept past like fire in a field of grain. Discouraged men felt the bracing influence and stimulant on the one side. On the other, it seemed that at last the billows of the ocean had broken upon them, and they must yield or be forever overwhelmed. As each new regiment came up, with its shout and wild, eager dash in the face of the enemy, the ground was being gathered in like thread on a great spool as it revolves. Inch by inch the line yielded. The river was left behind, with its horrible secret, to keep its bloody tryst with the sea: to carry its drift of gallant men, who would, alas, be gallant no more, on the infinite wanderings of its waves, as they ran and struggled in vain to leave behind the memory and the burden of the pitiless struggle and carnage—the relics of man's power and courage and savagery, to do and to die by and for his fellow-man, that he may adjust differences he himself has raised from the infinite depths of his own ignorance—from the blindness of his benighted past! And still the river ran on in its hopeless effort, for the human drift kept pace, and the awful battle was lost and won. Shiloh had passed into history, and Grant was famous! The country took stock of its loss and its gain. One more milestone in the devious road was past. One more reef was taken in the irrepressible conflict. The North rejoiced. The South sorrowed, and mothers, wives, sisters, and sweethearts stared at the wall and wept and moaned for the treasure that was lost, for the price that was paid, and took up anew their stunned and silent part, and waited and hoped and prayed.

One of the first regiments to dash past into the hell of shot and shell was Beverly's. He had noticed, as people will notice trivial things in the midst of great crises, a board nailed to a tree. When the battle was over he had searched for his brother's regiment. At last he had found it, but Roy was not there. Some one said he had fallen, others said he had been captured just before the relief came—" Right up there by the challenge—by the tree." Beverly rode back toward the hill, sick and faint at heart. He wondered, with a thrill of superstitious fear, if that board was to be a sort of grave-mark for his brother, and if that was the reason he had noticed the ridiculous challenge at such a time. He would go back to the mark and search for his brother. He got down from his horse and tied him to the tree. The challenge was still there. He had no heart to read it, but started on his sickening search. Face after face that he knew—boys from the old college—looked up at him—some, alas, with stark, unseeing eyes, and others who begged for help. Boys he had in the old days cared for with youthful fervor, and yet they seemed as nothing to him now ; he must not lose time—he must find his brother. Again and again he turned a bloody face upward only to exclaim, "Thank God!" when he did not know the features. Oh, the infinite selfishness of Love! The toy it makes of our human sympathies! The contraction it puts upon our generosity of soul! The limitations it sets upon our helpfulness! When twilight came Beverly was still searching for his brother, and thanking God, in the face of every mangled form, that it was the face of some other man's brother—some other mother's son! He returned to the camp for a light. He could not wait until morning to be sure that Roy was captured. He hoped and prayed that it might be so, but he must know. No report had come to the regiment. Roy had not been found or recognized. Beverly went hastily through the hospital tents. Roy had not been brought in. The search on the field began again—the search for his brother. The relief corps were working heroically. Men with stretchers passed and repassed him, and still Beverly looked in vain. He turned his dark lantern on the stretchers as they approached him, and sighed with relief as each passed on. He came to the spot where the little church had stood, now dismantled and wrecked by shell.

One after another he turned the faces of prostrate men upward. The night was wearing on. He was desperate, discouraged, and yet he had begun to settle into a solid hope that Roy had been captured and taken back into the Confederate ranks before the relief had come. He was making his way back to the tree and his impatient horse, when he heard a gurgling groan in a muddy ravine through which the retreating cannon had gone. He turned aside and searched with his lantern again. Deep in the stiff mud lay a young officer. His legs were deeply imbedded. Evidently the wheel of a cannon-carriage, or some other heavy wheel, had passed over him and crushed his legs into the soft earth. He had lain directly in the path of the retreating ordnance. The deep tracks told where the wheels had been. Beverly turned sick. He stooped to lift the face that lay half in the mud and water.

"Oh, Roy! Roy! my brother!" he gasped and fell upon his knees. His hand trembled so that the canteen fell from his grasp. He groped for it as the lantern lay beside him, and one hand still held the face above the earth. "Roy!

Roy! can you hear me? Can you hear me? It is your brother! It is Beverly!" he cried out, but for reply there was only that gurgling groan, followed by another and another—and then silence.

"Oh, my God!" cried Beverly. "What can I do? It will kill him to try to lift those poor crushed legs and——"

The light fell on the breast, and there, for the first time, Beverly saw that it was not mud alone that lay there, but that a piece of spent shell was half crushed into Roy's side. It was plain now. Roy had fallen with that, and the retreating battery had driven over his helpless form. Beverly wiped the mud and powder from his brother's face and bent down and kissed the parted lips.

"Oh, my brother! my brother! I came too late at last! I thought all the way on the river, and then, as we dashed up that hill, I thought we had come in time to save you, and I was so glad! Roy, I prayed not to be too late! Somehow I thought you were up there. And you were here—here, with this ghastly wound—and they drove over you! O, Roy, Roy, my brother, how can I ever tell mother? How can I?"

The long, gurgling moan came again. Beverly sprang to his feet and shouted for help. Shout after shout rang out. At last a reply came, and then men with a stretcher.

"I have found my brother," was all Beverly could say. His own voice seemed strange and distant to him. The men set about lifting the body from its bed of clay—the body of this spruce young officer who had been so eager that his brother should feel proud to see him in his new uniform with the first-lieutenant's straps! No one could tell what the uniform was now, and the jaunty cap and polished sword were gone! The strong young legs and the erect figure could boast of its extra inch no longer. Beverly breathed hard as the men worked. "I'm afraid he's too far gone to help now, captain. It——"

"Oh, let *me* lift his head! I can't pull on those poor crushed legs! Be so careful! Oh, God! oh, God! how cruel! Be so careful!—oh, Roy! Roy!—We are trying to be so careful, Roy! We try not to hurt you so! My God, how cruel! I cannot bear it, brother!"

The body was on the stretcher at last, and

Beverly was wiping great beads of anguish from his own face. One poor leg was crushed near the hip, and had been hard to manage. The groans had become more distinct and frequent. Then, "Dr—dr," came from the lips.

"Here, here, give me a canteen! I lost mine down there. Quick, he wants a drink, I think. Here, brother Roy." Beverly put a hand under his head. "Here, Roy, dear, can you swallow? Oh, it hurts him so! Here, brother, *my* brother! Oh, Roy, I wish it were I! Can you hear me? Can you hear me, Roy?"

The men with the stretcher turned their faces away and drew their sleeves across their eyes. Even they who had worked all night with and for the dead and dying were moved anew by the young officer's sorrow. Beverly looked up hopefully.

"I think he swallowed just a little. Let us get him to a surgeon, quick. Perhaps, perhaps——" Beverly looked from one to the other and could not finish his sentence. The little group moved wearily toward the hospital tents, and Beverly ran for the surgeon of his own company.

"My God, doctor, he has been driven over, and he is wounded in the breast besides! Do you think there is any hope? Oh, how I wish it were I! Oh, doctor, can't you save him? It is my brother—my brother Roy!"

The surgeon was listening as he worked.

"The best thing that could have happened to him is that he was so deep in that mud. It has kept the fever down. It has saved his leg. It isn't badly swollen. I can set this bone. I don't think the other one is——" He was examining and talking slowly. He changed to the wound in the breast. "This is the most—this is the worst, but I don't think the lung is badly—this plaster of mud on his breast——"

"I took it nearly all off, doctor. It was very thick when I found him, and this——" Beverly took a large jagged piece of shell from his pocket. "This was down in it. I think it must have struck and stunned him, and while he was helpless those cruel wheels went over him. His body was as if he had fallen on his back, but the legs were twisted as if he had been on his side. The mud was nearly two feet deep. It was an awful place, awful! And to think that they should have driven over Roy! Do you think——?"

"That was the best place he could have been. That mud has acted like——" The doctor was taking professional pride in the case. The wounded man groaned.

"Oh, how it seems to hurt him, doctor! Can't you—can't I—couldn't we give him something to deaden—? He was never so strong as I. He——"

"You'd better go away, captain. You're brave enough for yourself, but you'd better go away. I'll do my level best for him. I don't think this wound is fatal — and the mud poultice was the very best thing that could have happened to him, really. The wheel that threw that did him a greater service than it did injury to his leg. I—you had better go and lie down for a while, captain. I'll do everything possible, and—well, I hope his lung is not very seriously implicated. I hope we can pull him through. I feel sure of the leg and—go and lie down. You can't do any good here, and you mustn't lose your nerve that way. If he—if I—if he regains consciousness I'll call you. Try to get a little rest for to-morrow. Try. You may be needed then. You must have your nerve then, too, if he should open his eyes and——"

"*If* he should open his eyes!" Beverly turned away and sat with his face in his hands. "How can I write it to mother," he moaned—"how can I? How can I? And father may not be there to help her bear it! Oh, Roy, Roy, my brother!"

CHAPTER XIX.

"How dear to my heart are the scenes of my childhood."

WHEN the news of the battle reached Katherine, she was still alone. Griffith had not completed the task set, and was still in the tent of the irascible General, whose chief acquaintance with the English language appeared to lie in his explosive and ever ready profanity. He swore if things went right, and he swore if they went wrong. If he liked a man, he swore at him playfully, and if he disliked him, he swore at him in wrath. His ammunition might give out, but a volley of oaths was never wanting to fire at the enemy. It sometimes seemed to Griffith the irony of fate that he should be placed in the same tent and closely associated with such a man, for, although Griffith said nothing, it grated sadly upon his ears, and he sometimes wondered if the Almighty would prosper an expedition led by this man, for Griffith had kept still, through all the years the primitive idea of a personal God who takes cognizance of the doings of men, and meets and parries them by devices and schemes of His own.

As time went on, and Lengthy Patterson recovered from his wound so as to be always in evidence, he came in for a large share of the General's explosive and meaningless oaths. Sometimes it was half in fun, more often it was in memory of the fact that Lengthy had ignored him and his questions upon their first meeting, and that up to this day the lank mountaineer took his orders and his cue from Griffith only. He had attached himself to the sharpshooters and rarely left Griffith's side. As silent and faithful as a dog he rode day after day, with watchful eyes, by the side of or just behind " the Parson," as he still called the object of his adoration. He watched Griffith narrowly. He noticed the growing sadness of the old-time merry face. He felt that something was wrong. At last the silence could be preserved no longer, he must know what the trouble was. They were near the borders of the county where Griffith's old home was. Lengthy had expected to see his face grow interested and bright, but instead there seemed to come over it a drawn and haggard look that was a puzzle and a torment to the woodsman. He ventured a remark as they rode apart from the rest.

"Sick?"

"No, no, Lengthy. I'm not sick. Why?"

"Yeh never talk no mo'. Heard yeh kinder groan. Few-words-comprehends-th'-whole."

Griffith turned his face full upon him.

"Lengthy, it is almost more than I can bear to do this work. I—it is—sometimes I think I *cannot* take them over there." He held out his hand toward the beautiful valley in the distance. They could see the thread of the river winding through the trees and out into field and farm. It was the river in which Lengthy had seen this friend of his baptized, so many years ago, when both were young men, and now both were growing gray!

Lengthy made no reply. The silence stretched into minutes. They halted for the noon meal and to feed and rest the horses. They all lay about on the hill, and Griffith talked to the engineers. They drew lines and made figures and notes. An hour later they pushed on toward the river. Lengthy and Griffith rode in front. The old mill where Pete had run away appeared in the distance. The river was very near now. A heavy sigh from Griffith broke the silence. He was looking far ahead and his face was drawn and miserable.

"What d' yeh go fer?"

Griffith did not hear. His chin had dropped upon his breast, and his face was pale. His lips moved, and the mountaineer waited. At last he said: "What yeh do hit fer?"

"What?"

"What yeh do hit fer, 'f yeh don't want teh?"

"Do what? Go here?"

"Yeh?".

"I am a Union man, Lengthy. The President sent for me and asked me to do it. He made me see it was my duty. There was no one else he could trust, who knew the country. I——" There was a long pause. The mountaineer threw his leg up over the front of his saddle, and ruminated on the new outlook. Presently Griffith went on: "Some one *must* do it, but——" He lifted his face toward the blue above him:

"Oh, my God, if this cup could but pass from me!" he groaned aloud. "It seems to me I cannot cross that river! It seems to me I *cannot!*" His voice broke and there was silence.

"Don't need teh."

Griffith did not hear. His eyes were closed and he was praying for light and leading, as he would have called it—for strength to do the dreaded task, if it must be done. Lengthy looked at him, and then at the not far distant river, and waited in silence. A half mile farther on he said, as if the chain of remarks had been unbroken: "Don't need teh cross. I will fer yeh."

"What?" cried Griffith, like a man who has heard and is afraid to believe.

"Said yeh didn't need teh cross. I will fer yeh. Few-words-comprehends-th'-whole," he repeated, in the same level key, looking straight at his horse's ears.

Griffith's bridle fell upon his horse's neck. Both arms lifted themselves up, and both hands spread as if to grasp something. "Oh, my God, is my prayer to be answered so soon? Do you mean—oh, Lengthy, do you mean that you will save me from this terrible trial? Do you mean——"

"I does." He was gazing straight ahead of him now, with elaborate pretense of indifference. He had begun to grasp the situation.

Griffith dropped both hands upon his uplifted face, and a cry as of one in great pain escaped him, "O-h-h," in a long quaver. The mountaineer turned his eyes. Griffith was looking straight at him now, like a hunted man who at last sees hope and rescue ahead, but dares not trust it lest it prove but an illusion. He tried to speak, but his voice failed him. The mountaineer understood.

"Yeh kin go home. I'll do hit. Few words——"

Griffith was overtaken with hysterics. He threw both arms above his head and shouted, "Glory to God in the highest! Peace and good will to men!" and covered his face with his hands to hide the emotion he could not control. They were on the banks of the river now, and the commander dashed up. "What in hell's the matter now?" he demanded.

"Hit's the river done it," put in the mountaineer, to save his friend the need of words. "Baptized thar."

"What? What in the devil are you talking about? What in——"

He was looking at Griffith, but Lengthy broke in again with his perfectly level and emotionless voice. "Baptized thar, I sez. Few-words-comprehends-th'——"

"Will you dry up? You infernal—— What does this mean?" He turned again to Griffith, who had regained his self-control. The commander usually acted upon him as a refrigerator, so incapable was he of understanding human emotion that reached beyond the limits of irritability.

"General," he began, slowly, "I have just arranged with Mr. Patterson for him to take my place as Government Guide. I can go with you no farther. That house over there in the distance"—he stretched out his hand—"used to be my old home. I love the people who live here—all about here. This river——"

A volley of oaths interrupted Griffith. The command had come up, and the staff-officers sat listening and waiting. The General was changing his first outburst into arguments. Griffith met them quite calmly. It seemed a long time now since he had found the relief he felt. It did not seem possible that it was only ten minutes ago that it had come to him.

"This man knows the country even better than I do, General. He is willing to go—to take my place—and he is perfectly loyal—*loyal to me.* He will—what Mr. Lincoln wanted was that the work should be done, and done by one he could trust—it was not that he wanted *me* to do it. I will stake my honor on this man's fidelity. He——" The word "deserter," mingled with threats, struck Griffith's ear; he did not pause to analyze it. "Mr. Lincoln told me that I was to return to him whenever I——"

"God damn Mr. Lincoln! *I* am in command of these troops! Mr. Lincoln didn't know he was giving me a couple of lunatics to deal with! If you attempt to leave you will be shot as a deserter, I tell you! I'll do it myself, by God!"

Griffith's head dropped against his breast. He dismounted slowly and handed his bridle to the mountaineer. Lengthy hooked it over his arm and waited. Mr. Davenport deliberately knelt by the bank of the river, with his face toward the old home.

"Shoot. I will go no farther!" he said, and closed his eyes.

Instantly the mountaineer's gun went to his shoulder. His aim was at the General's breast. "Few-words-comprehends-th'-whole," he said, and the hammer clicked. The General smiled grimly.

"Get up," he said. "I had no right to make that threat. You are a private citizen. You came of your own accord. You *are* under Lincoln only. Get up! Can we trust this man, damn him?"

Griffith staggered to his feet. The storm had left him weak and pale. The mountaineer dismounted and stood beside him.

"You mean to take my place in good faith— to lead them right—I know, Lengthy; but tell him so *for me*," Griffith asked, in a tired voice, taking the swarthy hand in his. "You will do your best as a guide in my place, won't you?"

Lengthy's response was unequivocal. "I will," he said in his monotonous tone, and somehow, as they stood hand in hand with the curious group of men about them, the reply reminded every one of the response in the marriage service, and a smile ran around as the men glanced at each other.

"You promise to do all in your knowledge and power to enable them to get accurate knowledge and make their maps, don't you, Lengthy?"

"I do."

The similitude struck even the commander, and when Griffith turned, the irascible General was trying to cover a smile.

"Are you satisfied, General? I will stake my life on both his capacity to do it—even better than I—and on his honor when he promises to do it for me. Are you satisfied?"

"Have to be satisfied, I guess. Mount! March!"

Griffith lifted the hard, brown, rough hand in both of his and gravely kissed it. "You are the truest friend I ever had, Lengthy. God bless and protect you! Good-bye."

The mountaineer laid the great hand on the palm of its fellow, and looked at it gravely as he rode.

"Kissed it, by gum!" He gazed at the spot in silent awe. "Few-words-comp——" His voice broke, and he rode away at the head of the command, still holding the sacred hand on the palm of the one not so consecrated, and looked at it from time to time with silent, reverential admiration. His gun lay across his saddle, and the horse took the ford as one to the manner born. On the farther bank he turned and looked back. Griffith waved his handkerchief, and every man in the command joined in the salute when Lengthy's shout rang out, "Three cheers for the Parson!"

Even the General's hat went up, and Griffith rode back alone over the path he had but just come, alone—and unguarded—but with a great load lifted from his shoulders, bound for Washington to make his final report to the President, and then return to the ways and haunts of peace.

"Homeward bound! homeward bound! thank God!" he said, aloud, "with life's worst and hardest duty done. Surely, surely, my part of this terrible struggle is over! It has shadowed me for twenty long years. The future shall be free. Peace has come for me at last!"

CHAPTER XX.

"The days of youth are the days of gladness."

"Dear Mother," wrote Howard, "I forgot to write last week, but then there wasn't the first thing to tell, so it don't matter. We're just loafing here in camp waiting for the next move. We had a little scrap with the Johnnies ten days ago, but it didn't come to anything on either side. They are sulking in their tents and we are dittoing in ours. But what I began this letter to tell is really funny, and I don't want to forget to write it. The other day a slabsided old woman (you never did see such a funny looking creature. She was worse than the mountaineer class in Virginia, or even than those Hoosiers out there on that farm near ours.) Well, she came to our camp from some place back in the country and asked to see our 'doctor man.' She seemed to think there was but one.

One of the surgeons had a talk with her, and it turned out that her 'ole man,' as she called her husband, was 'mighty bad off with breakbone fever,' and she had come to see if the Yankee doctor man wouldn't have some kind of stuff that would cure him the first dose. These kinds of folks think our officers and doctors are about omnipotent, because our men are so much better fed and clothed and equipped than the Johnnies are.

"'Ef yoh can't gimme sumpin' fer my ole man, doctah, he's jes boun' ter die,' she kept saying over and over. Well, the doctor questioned her, and came to the conclusion that a good sweat would be about the proper caper to recommend, and he told her to cover him up well, and then to take some sage—they all have that in the garden and mighty little else—and, said he, 'take about so much and put it in something and then measure out exactly one quart of water and boil it and pour over the sage. Then make him drink it just as hot as he can. Now don't forget, so much sage and exactly a quart of water.'

"'Yeh think thet's agoin' t' cuah (cure) my ole man, doctah?' says she.

"'I think it is the best thing for him now. Be sure to make it as I told you—so much sage and a quart of water.'

"'You kin bet I'll fix her up all right, doctah, ef thet's a goin' t' cuah my ole man.' Then she tramped back home. The next day she appeared bright and early, and wanted that doctor man again. 'Well, my good woman, I hope your husband is feeling a good deal easier after his sweat. I——'

"'Naw 'e hain't nuther. My ole man, he hain't scooped out on the inside like you Yanks is, I reckon.'

"She looked pretty worried. 'How's that? How's that?' asked the doctor.

"'Wal,' says she, 'I jest hoofed hit home es quick es ever I could, an' I tuck an' medjured out thet there sage an' the water—jest edzactly a quat—an' I fixed her up an tuck hit t' the ole man. I riz his head up, mister—fer he's powerful weak—an' he done his plum best t' swaller hit, but the fust time he didn't git mo'n halft down till he hove the hull of hit up agin. I went back and I medjured up thet there sage agin an' the water an' tried him agin, but he hove her up *'fore* he got halft down. But I never stopped till I tries her agin, an' that time, doctah, he didn't *git* halft down. Now, doctah, thet there ole man er mine he don't *hold* but a pint. I reckon you Yanks is scooped out thinner than what we alls is.'

"We boys just yelled, but the poor soul loped off to her pint-measure old man without seeing a bit of fun in it. She was mad as a wet hen when the doctor told her she needn't make him drink it all at one fell swoop. She vowed he had told her that the first time, and it's my impression that she now suspects the Yankees of trying to burst her old man. I've laughed over it all day, so I thought I'd write it to you, but it don't seem half so funny in writing as it was to hear it.

"Give little Margaret this ring I put in. I cut it out of a piece of laurel root. I expect it is too big for her, but she can have some fun with it I reckon. There isn't any more news, only one of our cannons exploded the other day. It didn't do much damage. I'm not sure that I've spelled some of these words right, but my unabridged is not handy and I'm not sorry.

I always hated to look for words. I wish you'd tell some of the town boys to write to me. Letters go pretty good in camp and some fellows get a lot. I don't get many. It's hard to answer them if you get many, though, so I don't know which is worst. This is the longest one I ever wrote in my life. I forgot to tell you to tell Aunt Judy I met a fellow from Washington and he said the twins were in jail, but they were let out to work on some Government intrenchments near by. I don't know what they were in for. The fellow didn't know about our other niggers. Said he thought Mark and Phillis were dead because he used to see them but hadn't for a long time. Said Sallie worked for his mother sometimes and that is how he knew so much about them. Two or three of the boys got shot last night putting cartridges in the fire to monkey with the other fellows. None of 'em hit yours truly. My hand is plum woah out, as Aunt Judy would say, holding this pen—and the thing has gone to walking on one leg. I guess I broke the point off the other side jabbing at a fly. Good-bye. Write soon,

"HOWARD.

"P.S.—I forgot to say I am well, and send love. I wish I had some home grub.

"Foxy Leathers got a bully box last week. He gave me nearly half of his fruit cake. The other boys didn't know he had one. They got doughnuts—but even doughnuts are a lot better than the grub we get.   H."

The box of "home grub," was speedily packed and sent, and while it lasted it made merry the hearts of his mess. Howard said in one of his letters that he was growing very tall. He said that the boys declared that "if it had not been for his collar he would have been split all the way up, as he had run chiefly to legs." Howard, however, expressed it as his own unbiased opinion that it was jealousy of his ability to walk over the fences that they had to climb which prompted the remark. "Foxy has to climb for it and I put one leg over and then I put the other over—and there you are," he said. Camp life agreed with him, and the restraints of home no longer rasping his temper, he seemed to be the gayest of the gay. Nothing troubled him. He slept and ate wherever and whenever and whatever fell to his lot; lived each day as it came and gave no thought to its successor. He counted up on his fingers when he wrote home last, and tried to remember to write about once a week, because his mother begged that he would, and not at all because the impulse to do so urged him or because he cared especially to say anything. He liked to get letters, but he knew he was sure of those from home whether he wrote or not, and so his replies had that uncertainty of date dependent upon luck. No sense of responsibility weighed upon him, and his mother's anxiety impressed him— when he thought of it at all—as a bit of womanish nonsense; natural enough for a woman, but all very absurd. He had no deeper mental grasp upon it, and indeed the whole ethical nature of this boy seemed embryonic; and so it was that his camp life was the happiest he had ever known—the happiest he would ever know.

CHAPTER XXI.

> . . . "Consider, I pray,
> How we common mothers stand desolate, mark,
> Whose sons, not being Christs, die with eyes turned away,
> And no last word to say!"
>
> *Mrs. Browning.*

"DEAR LITTLE MOTHER," wrote Beverly. "When I telegraphed you last night that Roy was wounded and that I was safe and unhurt, I feared that to-day this letter would take you most terrible news—you who have the hardest part to bear, the silent, inactive part of waiting and uncertainty and inaction and anxiety—but to-day I feel so relieved that I can send you a very hopeful letter. The doctor says that Roy will surely live; and he hopes that the wounds will not prove so serious as we feared at first and as they looked. A piece of shell struck him in the breast but it must have been a spent shell, for although the place is considerably crushed in, the doctor now feels certain that no very serious damage is done his lung. That was what we feared at first. One of his legs is broken near the hip, but it is set and the doctor says it is doing well and will do so, for there is almost no fever. The great mud poultice that was on it for several hours at first was his salvation, so the surgeon thinks. I will not stop to explain this to you now, but when Roy gets home he will tell you, for he remembers most of it and we will tell him the rest. But just now I want simply to tell you the reassuring things and the plans I have made for Roy. He is perfectly conscious and says that he does not suffer very much. We don't allow him to talk, of course, for fear of his lung, but I've arranged to have him sent to Nashville, where he can be nursed as well as if he were at home. I recalled that the Wests live there now, and I sent a telegram asking if they would not take Roy to their house and care for him until we could send him home. They wired that they would be most happy to do so. You will recall that pretty little Emma West who used to come to the house. She was at school with Roy before he went to college. They are nice people, and

I am sure that Roy will be cared for as if he were their own. They are Union people. They will write to you daily, too, so that everything will be made as easy for you as possible. This takes a great load off my heart, and as Roy seems so bright to-day I am almost gay after yesterday's terrible experience—of which I shall tell you when we all get home, but not now. One of the most absurd things I ever heard of was that the very first question Roy tried to ask, when he became conscious, was who got the challenge last. It was a side challenge of battle between his regiment and a Louisiana regiment. It was posted on a tree—written on a slab of wood. I had tied my horse to that tree when I was looking for Roy, and had utterly forgotten him. Roy's question recalled the poor horse to me and I went to see what had become of him. There the old fellow stood, pawing the ground and twisting about the tree, hungry and thirsty and tired. He had knocked the challenge down and split it with his stamping feet. I gathered it up and took it to Roy, and a real lively smile crossed his face, and immediately he fell asleep. What strange freaks of fancy and of desire and ambition we are! I am told that Roy was promoted again on the field just before he was shot, so he is as big a captain now as I am, but that fact has not yet appeared to come back to him. Who got the challenge at the last was his first thought! I suspect he was thinking of that when he fell, and his returning consciousness took up the thread of thought right where he had dropped it or where it was broken by the lapse. It has not seemed to surprise him to see me. He acts as if I had been about him all along, and yet it has been nearly two years since we were together! Of course I act the same way so as not to excite him. He has had two long, good, natural naps to-day and I talked to him between. He knows he is to go to Nashville, and I had a sneaking idea that when I mentioned Emma West he looked uncommonly well pleased with the scheme. Do you know whether they got 'spoony,' after I left home? Anyhow that Nashville scheme seems to suit him all the way through. I feel absolutely light-hearted and gay to-day, mother mine. It is the reaction from the strain of yesterday and last night, I suppose; but if I could, I'd dance or sing or something. Since I can't do that I'll content myself with writing you rather a frivolous letter. You just ought to see these trees! They are simply riddled with shot and shell. This shows, too, one very good reason why so few of the rounds of ammunition take effect in the men. They shoot entirely too high. Quite above the heads of the tallest men. The trees are simply cartridge cases, and the limbs are torn away. The mud! You ought to see it. You'd think you never saw mud before. It took sixteen mules and the entire regiment hitched to one of the cannon to pull it along the road the Johnnies retreated over. A man we captured was one who had given out at the job. Poor fellows! they had a hard time of it all around, and we fresh troops who landed from the gunboats were the last straw in their cup of tribulation. I reckon they don't think they got their tribulation through a straw though, and the figure is a trifle mixed; but as a soldier I can't stop to edit copy! Oh, mother, I wish I could make you feel as relieved as I do to-day. Skittish is the word—I feel really skittish;

because I am so sure Roy is in no danger. I believe he will be able to go home before many weeks, and meantime, for all comforts, he will be as if he were at home. When he comes you can get the whole story of his fall, the fight, and his promotion. Dear old fellow! He's a great big captain now, and I stick right there. I'm acting Inspector-General now on the staff, but I'm really only a captain yet. I hope things will settle down before I get any higher— though I'd feel uncommonly well to have the same kind of a promotion as he got yesterday. I'm going to let him tell you himself. It was quite dramatic, as the fellows tell me. I just stopped to take a peep at him and he is sleeping like a baby. There is almost no fever. I feel like hugging this pottery clay mud—for we have it to thank for a good deal—but it makes us swear to march through it. I do hope father is home now. He is my main anxiety. I hope he won't see the papers if anything was said of Roy. He was thought to be ' missing,' at first when the reports went, and then to be killed; but don't worry a single bit. I am telling you the *very truth* when I tell you that last night I believed that Roy could not live and to-night I feel absolutely safe about him—I feel like singing—and all this accounts for this very giddy and jerky letter. I suppose I am what you'd call hysterical. Of course he will need intelligent care, but since that is all arranged for I shall march away to Corinth (that is our next aim) with a light heart and as hopeful as I want to make you feel. Ah, mother mine, I realize more and more what all this must be to you! I thought of it as I looked for Roy last night. Silent, patient, inactive anxiety! The part of war the women bear is by far the harder part. It takes bravery, of course, to face bullets and death; but it must require almost inspired heroism to sit inactively by and wait for it to strike those we love far better than life. More and more, small mother, do I realize this, do I understand that the hardest part of war *must* be borne by those who are not warriors; but we love you, little mother, and we will be as careful of the sons you care for and love as we can be and do our duty. We will not be foolhardy nor reckless, for your sake—*be sure*.

"One of the pathetic things that is not unmingled with humor was told me to-day by the young fellow in the next bed to Roy. He is a pretty boy, only about eighteen. He belongs to an Ohio regiment. During the first day's fight he got separated from his command and did not know whether he was inside or outside of our lines. He was picking his way around, peering from behind trees cautiously, trying to get his bearings, when all of sudden he came upon a Johnnie. Both were taken by surprise. The other fellow jumped and seemed about to shoot, and the Ohio boy yelled out, 'Don't shoot! don't shoot! I'm already wounded!'

"The Johnnie was a mere slip of a boy himself, and hadn't the faintest desire to shoot. They had both seen all they wanted to of war. Both were homesick and heartsick with it all. They sat down on a log and fell to comparing notes. Neither one knew whether he was captured or whether he had a prisoner. Both were lost. They agreed to call it even and go their separate ways when they got their bearings. Neither wanted to be a prisoner. 'I've got a dear old father back in Alabama, and if I ever see his face again I'll have enough sense to stay at home;' explained Johnnie, with a suspicious quaver in his voice. Ohio had the very dearest and best of fathers too, and he confessed that if he could but see his face now heaven would be his. They shook hands over the situation and both fell to crying softly, as they decided that war was not what it was cracked up to be. The two homesick fellows sat there on that log and compared notes about those blessed fathers at home, and both were blubbering—because they *had*, instead of because they had not, fathers who loved them and whom they loved! Well, the upshot was that they agreed to part friends; and go back to their regiments as soon as ever they could find out which one was captured. They'd just call it even and let each other off. The Ohio boy is laid up now with a Minie in his arm that he caught the next day, and he is wondering if the Alabama lad with the father sent him that ball as a keepsake and a reminder! So you see there are some humorous sides to these horrors after all, mother. My journalistic instinct has kept me amused with this thing a good deal to-day. I'd have given a good deal to have overheard the talk. I swear

I wouldn't have captured Alabama. He should have had his chance to go back to the dear old home and the father. Ohio was troubled over it, but I told him that he did exactly right. But wasn't it delightfully funny? Oh, mother mine, I wish I could say something to make you keep up good heart. I hope father is home. If I could be sure that he is, I'd feel almost gay, to-day. Wool little Margaret's curly pate for me and tell her that I say her chirographical efforts are very creditable for a young lady of her limited experience. Get her some little paper and encourage her to write to me often. It will do her good, and it will be a delight to me. Her last letter was as quaint and demure as her little self. Love to aunt Judy—the faithful old soul, and to the gentle Hosanna—in the highest —peace and good will; not to ·mention me re-spheets.'

"Keep up a brave heart, mother. It can't last much longer; and truly, truly I believe that Roy is *quite* safe. Kiss yourself for your eldest and loving son,

"BEVERLY."

CHAPTER XXII.

"Thy brother's blood the thirsty earth hath drunk."
Shakespeare.

WHEN Griffith reported at the White House, the President expressed himself as entirely satisfied. "You have done all I asked;" he said. "The maps sent, so far, are wonderfully fine and accurate, I can see that, and now that you have left a man who is able and willing to take your place, that is all I ask. If he should fail us I will send for you again; but I hope I shall not need to do that. If he is faithful, you have, indeed, done your whole duty, nobly. I thank you! I thank you! You are a silent hero—a war hero in times of peace and a peace hero in times of war! I am glad you can go home now. I—I happened to read—I always notice your name, now when I see it and——"

Griffith looked at him steadily. There was

evidently something bearing on the mind of the President which had to do with Griffith. Mr. Lincoln was moving toward the table. "Have you read—I suppose you have not seen the papers lately?"

"Nothing," Griffith said, shaking his head. "What is the news, Mr. Lincoln?"

"Glorious news! A great victory at Shiloh! A *great* victory; but——"

He turned over several papers and took one up from among the rest.

"What regiments are your sons in?" he asked, looking down the columns.

Griffith put out his hand. "What is the name, Mr. Lincoln? Is he killed or——"

The President retained the paper and feigned to be looking for a name. "No, no, missing—according to one account. The other—the news is too meager yet to—it is confused. We can't be sure, and then this paper is several days old, beside. I've seen nothing since—nothing at all of him. Here—Roy. Captain Roy Davenport of——"

"Roy is not a captain. That is his brother—Beverly. Is Roy——"

"He was promoted on the field, just before he fell—or—— This paper——"

Griffith staggered toward the door.

"I must go home. Just before he fell! Poor Katherine! Poor Roy! I must go home. I must make haste. How long——When did you say it was? When——?"

"Wait," said Mr. Lincoln. "Let me try for a message—for accurate news for you. Wait." He rang. "Send that message, instantly—to Shiloh—to the Colonel of the—— Indiana Infantry, and bring me the reply. Be quick—quick as you can," he said; and the secretary hastened away.

Silence fell between them. Griffith's hand reached out toward the paper Mr. Lincoln had let fall, but the long angular arm reached it first, and as if not noticing the movement of Mr. Davenport, he deftly slid it toward the pile of other papers, and then suddenly flung all into a confused heap as he searched for some article on the table.

"Would you like to go home that way?" They were both thinking of Shiloh, so why mention the name? "Perhaps if you did, you might find—you might take him home with you if——Have you wired his mother that *you* are safe, and here on your way home? That was right. That will help her to bear——" He arose restlessly and placed both hands upon Griffith's shoulders. "Mr. Davenport, I can't thank you enough for your services. I want you to understand that I *know* what it all meant to you, and that I appreciate it at its full value. I hope the time will come when you will let a grateful country know what you have done and—and——" He held out his hand for the message as the door had opened for the secretary. He read and turned the other side up, and then re-read it. "Who is Beverly? Colonel, of—Oh, your son? Oh, this is for you! I did not notice the address. I wondered who loved me!" Mr. Lincoln smiled as he handed the message to his guest. "Roy is wounded, but doing well. Have sent him to Nashville to the Wests. I am unhurt. I love you. Beverly," Griffith read. Then he took out his handkerchief and blew a great blast.

"Was there ever such a boy? To telegraph *that!*" He smiled up at Mr. Lincoln through proud dim eyes. "That is my oldest son—the Captain." The quaver in his voice and the smile in his eyes, drowned as it was in moisture, touched the great man before him, who took the message again and re-read it as Griffith talked. "He is a good son. He——"

"He loves you he says, and the other one is doing well. You ought to be satisfied. A good many fathers are not fixed just that way, to-day!" Mr. Lincoln shook his head sadly from side to side, and the tragic face sank into its depth of gloom again. "Too many fathers have no sons to love them to-day—too many, too many," he said gloomily. "When will it all end? How will it all end?" He held out the message as he suddenly turned to the table. "You will want to keep that. Do you want to go by way of Nashville, now? Or straight home?"

Griffith re-read the message. "Straight home," he said. "He is in good hands—and—and he is safe. Straight home." Then suddenly, as he folded the telegram and placed it in his inside pocket, "Mr. Lincoln, did you know I am a deserter?"

"What?"

"Did you know I deserted? The General threatened to shoot me, and——"

"W-h-a-t!"

Griffith told the story of the threat simply, fully. The keen eyes watched him narrowly. There was a growing fire in them.

"Didn't you know he couldn't shoot you? Didn't you know you were under *me?* Didn't you know——"

"I didn't think of that at first, Mr. Lincoln. I thought he could, and—I thought he would, for a little while. I was——"

"If he had," said the President, rising and showing more fire than he had exhibited before, "well, if he had, all I've got to say, is that there'd a' been two of you shot!" Then, recalling himself he smiled grimly. "If he does his share as well as you've done yours, I'll be satisfied."

"Before I go, Mr. Lincoln, I wanted to speak to you about a little matter. You said something just now about a grateful country, and—but—I recall that you—I understood you to— The fact is, when I was here before, I somehow got the idea that you were willing to—to pay, and to give a Colonel's commission, and—and emoluments—to one who could do this service, and——"

Mr. Lincoln dropped the hand he held, and an indescribable change passed over the tall form and the face, which made both less pleasant to see. But he smiled, as he passed his hand over his face, and turning toward the table with a tired expression, reached for a pen.

"You've sort of concluded that the job is worth pay, have you?"

"Yes, it's worth all you can afford to pay, Mr. Lincoln; it is extremely dangerous business. Is the offer still open?"

The President gave an imperceptible shrug to his loose shoulders, and drew a sheet of paper toward him.

"Certainly. Commission?" he said as he began to write.

"Yes, if you will. A Colonel's commission and pay dating all back to the beginning of my service—if that is right."

Mr. Lincoln nodded, but there was a distinctly chilly air creeping into his tone. "Y-e-s, of course. 'Nything else?"

"I don't see hardly how you can date it back either, without——"

"Oh yes, I can date it back to the beginning of your service," he said wearily, "but I don't know——"

"I guess you'll have to just put it Col. L. Patterson, for I don't know his real name, the baptismal one. Known him all my life just as Lengthy, but of course that won't——"

"What!" the President had turned to face him, but Griffith was still looking contemplatively out of the window, and did not notice the sudden change of tone and position.

"It will give him a certain standing with the men—and with the General—that he will need—and deserve, and—and—and the rest is right too, for *him*, if——"

Mr. Lincoln thrust his fingers back and forth through his already disheveled hair, and at last burst out: "Can't say that I exactly get your idea. I understood you to say that you had changed your mind about—about wanting the rank of Colonel, and—and the pay for——"

He was looking full at Griffith, and the preacher's eyes traveled back from the distant hills and fell upon the face before him. It struck him that the face looked tired and worn. He pulled himself up sharply, for the dull way he had been presenting the case, and his reply was in a fuller, freer voice, with a brisker air of attention to business.

"Certainly, certainly, Mr. Lincoln, that's it exactly." Then with a lowered voice: "Perhaps you don't realize, Mr. Lincoln, that every instant a man in that situation, who is known and recognized, and who holds no commission, and wears no federal uniform, has his life in his hands—is in more danger than any soldier ever is, and——"

"Realize! Didn't I tell you so? Didn't I ask you to go better protected? Didn't I——?"

Griffith waved his hand and went on.

"I somehow couldn't bring myself to take the attitude and position of a soldier. I am a man of peace, a non-combatant, a clergyman, and—and then there was some sort of sentiment —of—Mr. Lincoln, it isn't necessary to try to explain *my* position. The fact is, I doubt if I could, if I tried, make you understand wholly; but I want this Government to protect Lengthy Patterson with all the power and all the devices it has. And I want him to have a commission that will place him where he will receive respect and consideration in our own ranks; and if he is captured. I want money paid to him to live on afterward, if he should be hurt—and he can never live in his old home again. I want——" He had risen and was standing near the President again. His voice had grown intense in its inflection. "Lengthy Patterson has taken my place, and I want—and—if you will just give him all that—I don't see how you can date it back either, or he will suspect that *I* am paying him—and he wouldn't take a cent; but if—can't you just——"

A great gleam of light seemed to break over the rugged face of the President. He arose suddenly, and threw one arm around Griffith's shoulders, and grasped his hand again.

"God bless my soul! Certainly! Of course! By the lord Harry, I didn't understand you at first. I—— Why, certainly, the man who took your place shall have both the commission that will shield him and the pay he deserves, certainly, certainly!" They were moving toward the door. "Anything else, Mr. Davenport?"

"I reckon you will have to let him think that *I* took—that I was both commissioned and—and paid, Mr. Lincoln, or he won't take it—and—and there isn't the least reason why *he* should not. He *must*. Can I leave it all—will you see that——?"

"Oh, yes, yes, that's all right. I'll fix that—I'm glad it's that way——" He broke off and took Griffith's hand. "Well, good-bye. Good-bye. I hope, when we meet again, it will not be—I hope this war will be over, and that I shall have no more need to test men like you. But—ah, you have a son who loves you and the other one is safe! I wish to heaven all loyal men were as well off as you are to-night. I am glad for you, and yet I sometimes think I shall never feel really glad again," and the strong homely face sank from its gently quizzical smile into the depths of a mood which had come to be its daily cast. He stretched out his hand for another message, and stood reading it as

Griffith closed the door behind him. "New Orleans is ours," was all that the message said, but Mr. Lincoln sighed with relief and with pain. Victory was sweet, but carnage tortured his great and tender soul. The sadly tragic face deepened again in its lines, and yet he said softly, as he turned to his desk: " Thank God! Thank God! one more nail is driven into the coffin of the Confederacy. Let us hope that rebellion is nearly ready to lie down in it and keep still. Then perhaps we can be glad again —perhaps we can forget!"

CHAPTER XXIII.

"Through the shadows of the globe we sweep into the younger day."   *Tennyson.*

"WHEN the war is over and the boys all get home," Griffith was fond of saying, as he sat and talked with Katherine, "how good it will seem just to live! I've seen all the suffering and shadows of tragedy I want to see for my whole life. The boys and I will make it up to you, Katherine, and these gray hairs that have come," he touched the wavy hair with tender fingers, "these gray hairs that have come since we went away, shall be only memoranda of the past, not heralds of the future."

It was such infinite relief to have him at home and well that Katherine almost forgot for a time to feel troubled about her sons. News had come daily from the first about Roy; but now that he was so much improved the letters gradually grew a little less frequent. Sometimes Emma

West wrote them, and then the letters were very minute indeed, and full of anxious hopefulness. Her praise of Roy's fortitude, her descriptions of his wonderful courage and the insistence with which she assured Katherine that no duty of all their lives—her father's and mother's—had ever been done with half so hearty a good-will as was the nursing of the young Captain, had in it all a spirit of devotion and a guarded tenderness that Katherine thought she understood. Although it is true that no girl is ever quite good enough to marry any mother's son, Katherine tried to adjust herself with reasonable fortitude to the idea of what she thought she saw in the future. Of course it would be many years in the future before the finality must be faced, and Katherine was learning to live in the present and to push aside that which threatened or even promised, as too uncertain to dwell upon. At last short notes, and then longer ones, from Roy himself began to come, and the time seemed not far off when the invalid would arrive. It was wholly unlikely, he said, that he would be fit for service again during the war, unless the war should last much longer than his original term of enlistment and he should enlist again. Of his final recovery he felt certain. The crushed side was doing well, and he would be only slightly lame, the doctor said. To get him out of the army by even so heroic a process gave his mother comfort, and she felt that she could keep him out now even should he recover before his enlistment period were over, she would, if need be, appeal to Mr. Lincoln, and she felt sure, from all Griffith had told her, that the President would give Roy an honorable discharge. Two of her brood were safe again, she argued with herself, and meantime news from Howard and Beverly was frequent and assuring. Life seemed about to drop into less tragic lines in the little household. Griffith fell to humming his favorite hymns once more, and sometimes as he sat on the porch and watched or greeted the passers-by or read his paper, he would stop to tell Katherine stories of his recent adventures, where they did not trench too closely upon the sorrowful memories of the cold faces and bitter feelings of his one-time friends. To no one else did he speak of where he had been. His townsmen knew that he had been away, of course. The

Bishop and the college trustees alone knew why. To all others his few months' absence was no more significant than many another trip he had taken since he came among them. The duty he had felt forced to do had been too painful in its nature to make him willing to discuss it even after it was over. Most of those about him were bitter toward the South with a bitterness born of ignorance of conditions and of the times of excitement. To this man, who had passed through the fire before the general conflagration was kindled, there was no bitterness. He understood. His sympathy was still with those who were caught on the under side of the wheel of progress as it had revolved. His beliefs and convictions had long ago traveled with the advance line; but he left all sense of unkindness and revenge to those who were less competent to see the conflict from the side of understanding, and who judged it through the abundance of their ignorance and prejudice. To Griffith it was like watching the tide rise on the sea. It was unavoidable, and those who were caught out beyond the safety line were bound to go down. He did not blame the sea. He only deplored the inevitable loss, the sorrow, the suffering, and the mistakes which made it all possible. That his own part of it was in and of the past lightened his heart. One day as he sat listlessly on the side porch reading his Gazette, he noticed vaguely the half-witted girl, now almost grown to womanhood, circling about the gate and making aimless passes toward the end of the house. He watched her covertly over his paper for a moment and went on humming. "He leadeth me, oh, blessed thought!" The movements of the demented creature seemed to take on more definiteness. Griffith arose and stepped to the end of the porch. There sat aunt Judy, smoking her pipe, and swaying her body in time with his humming. "O words with heavenly comfort fraught! Where'er I go, whate'er I be,"—Griffith's step had attracted the old woman and she opened her eyes and looked up at him. "Still 'tis His hand that leadeth me," Griffith finished, smiling at her.

"Lawd amassy, honey, I des been a settin' heah wid my po' ole eyes shet, a listenin' to dat dar song er yoahrn! Hit sholy do seem des lack ole times come back agin t' heah yoh sing dat a way! Hit sholy do! Lawsy, honey, dey want no singin' 'roun' heah whilse you wus gone all dat long time. Dey want dat! Hit wus des dat gloomysome dat hit seem lack somebody daid *all* de time. Hit sholy do go good t' set heah an' listen ter yoh singin' agin! Hit sholy do, Mos' Grif." She suddenly looked toward the street. "Mos' Grif, what dat dare fool gal doin'? She des do like dat a way *all* de time. I hain't nebber seed her when she don't do des dat er way. I ax her wat she want, an I ax er wat ails 'er, an' she don't say nothin' 'tall. She des keep on doin' dat way."

"She's afflicted, aunt Judy. She's a poor afflicted creature and——"

"Lawsy, honey, *any*body kin see dat she's 'flicted; but wat I axes yoh is, what fer she do dat away at me? She ain' do dat a way at yoh, an' she ain' do dat a way at Mis' Kate—an' she ain' do dat a way at Mis' Marg'et, needer. Des at me. She tryin' ter witch me. Dat's what!"

Griffith laughed. The point of view was so unexpected and yet so wholly characteristic that it struck him as humorous beyond the average of aunt Judy's mental processes. His laugh rang out loud and clear. His broad shoulders shook. He had grown quite portly, and his face was the picture of health and fine vigor.

"What fer yoh laugh dat a way, Mos' Grif? Dat dar fool gal would a witched me long time ago if hit hadn't a been fer dat." She took from her bosom, where it hung from a string, the rabbit foot: "Dat's so. Des as sho' as yo' bawn, honey; dey ain' no two ways 'bout dat!"

The fascination of the strange black face for this clouded intellect seemed never to lose its power. Whenever and wherever Judy had crossed her path all else faded from the half vacant brain, and such mind and attention as there was, fixed itself upon the old colored woman. Judy had tried every art she possessed to engage the girl in conversation, but with no results. She would continue to circle about and make her passes of indirection with one hand outstretched and the other hung aimlessly pendent at her side in that helpless fashion which defies simulation. Judy had even tried threatening the girl with her cane; but no threat, no coaxing and no cajolery served to free her from this admirer who seemed transfixed as a bird is fascinated by a snake—with the fascination of perplexity and fear—in so far as the vacant soul could know such lively and definite sensations. Judy had finally—long ago—taken refuge in her rabbit foot, and made up her mind that in competition in the black art, only, was safety. She shook the foot at the girl, who responded in the usual fashion. How long the contest might have lasted it would be difficult to say, had not Griffith walked toward the gate. The instant the bulk of his body hid the old black woman from her eyes, nature did the rest. The vacant mind, no longer stimulated by the sight of the uncanny face, lost all interest and continuity of thought and wandered aimlessly on; forgetful alike of her recent object of attention and equally unguided by future intent, her steps followed each other as a succession of physical movements only, and had no object and no destination. Aimlessly, listlessly, walking; going no one knew where; thinking no one knew what—if, indeed, her poor vague mental operations might be classified as thought —living, no one knew why; following the path of least resistance, as how many of her betters have done and will do to the end of time: looking no farther than the scope of present vision; remembering nothing: learning nothing; an object of pity, of persecution, of fear or of aversion according as she crossed the path of civilized or savage, of intelligent and pitiful or of pitiless ignorance. Griffith watched her as she wove her devious way and wondered where, in the economy of Nature, such as she could find a useful place, and why, in the providence of God, she had been cast adrift to cumber the earth, to suffer, to endure and at last to die—where and why and how? He was not laughing as he returned to the house, and aunt Judy scanned his face narrowly, and then carefully replaced the rabbit foot in its resting-place in her bosom.

"Druv' er off. She know! *She* know a preacher o' de gospil o' de Lawd Jesus Chris' w'en she see 'um! Dey ain't no two ways 'bout dat—'flicted or no 'flicted. Dat dar gal's 'flicted o' course, but she know 'nuf ter know *dat!* She been tryin ter witch me, *dat* she is; but Lawd God A'mighty, she hain't got no sense, ter try ter witch *dis* house wid Mos' Grif an' dat rabbit foot *bofe* in hit! Dat dar gal's a plum bawn fool ter try dat kine er tricks. She is dat. She's wus dan 'flicted. She's a plum bawn ejiot ter try dat kine er tricks aroun' dese heah diggins. She is dat! Lawsy, Lawsy, she ain' got no sense worf talkin' 'bout! Mos' Grif an' dat rabbit foot bofe t' match up wid! Lawsy, Lawsy, dat dar pore 'flicted gal's a plum bawn fool!" And poor old aunt Judy, still talking to herself, hobbled into the house, satisfied with her estimate of all parties concerned and content with the world as she found it, so long as that world contained for her both a Mos' Grif and her precious rabbit foot.

White or black, bond or free, war or peace, were all one to old aunt Judy; nothing mattered in all this infinite puzzle called life, if but there remained to her these two strongholds of her faith and her dependence! And who shall say that aunt Judy was not wise in her day and generation? So wise was she that sorrow, anxiety, and care had passed her lightly by to the end that her eighty years sat upon her shoulders like a pleasant mantle, adjusted, comfortable to a summer breeze.

CHAPTER XXIV.

"And what are words? How little these the silence of the
    soul oppress!
Mere froth,—the foam and flower of seas whose hungering
    waters heave and press
Against the planets and the sides of night,—mute, yearn-
    ing, mystic tides!"

Bulwer.

"I AM coming home next month," wrote Roy, "with my wife—the very dearest, sweetest, most lovable and beautiful girl in the whole world. We have decided not to wait, but to be married at once—as soon as she can get ready, and I a bit stronger—and go home for our bridal trip. The winter at home with you will finish up my recovery (and if anything on earth could facilitate it, Emma's nursing and care and love will,) and then if the war is not over, of course I'll go back if I am needed—enlist again. My time is out now; but I hope and believe that the war will be over, or, at least, on its last legs by that time, and then I can begin business at once. My own idea is to take the stock-farm, if father is willing, instead of leaving it to those Martins who don't know the first thing about stock-breeding, and go in for fine horses and a few fine cows, too. I got hold of some books on those subjects here. Emma's father used to have a fancy that way, and I've read up and talked a lot with him on the subject in these four months. Don't you think we could fix the house out there on the place so it would do very well, indeed, for a couple of young folks who won't care so very much about anything at all but each other?"

Griffith stopped reading the letter to laugh.

"Tut, tut, tut! Here's more love in a cottage business for you. Well, well, I *am* surprised, Katherine! I am——"

"I am not. I've been expecting it all along—only—I did hope—I didn't think it would be quite so *soon*. Roy is only twen——"

"Well, well, 'pon my soul, it looks as if you didn't get out of one kind of a frying-pan in this world until you got into another. I was just building all sorts of castles about the future and -and to tell the mortal truth, Katherine, I never once thought of making a place for a daughter-in-law! Never once! Why——" There was a long pause. Griffith finished the letter in silence and handed it to his wife. As she read—she began back at the beginning—he gazed straight before him with unseeing eyes and a low hum ran along with unsteady and broken measure. "How tedious—mmmm—mm—the hours. Mmmmm—no longer mmmm mm : Sweet pros—mmm, swee—et mmm mm mm, mmmm, Ha—ave all mm mm mm mm to me.' But we'll have to expand the castle, Katherine—build on an addition for a daughter-in-law." he said as if there had been no break in the conversation, albeit almost half an hour had passed during which each had been wrapped in thought, and the singing—if Griffith's natural state of vocalization may be called by that name—was wholly unnoticed by both.

"Yes." said Katherine in a tired voice ; " yes, but I had hoped for a reunion of—of just ourselves first ; but—but—we will try to feel that she *is* one of ourselves—and surely we ought to be very grateful for the way they have nursed

Roy and—His letter——" Katherine fell to discussing his letter and the new plans and needs, and how short a time it would be until they would come.

Little Margaret hailed with delight the idea of a new sister. They all remembered the pretty face of the school-girl Emma. Letters of congratulation and welcome were written and posted, and it seemed to Katherine that nothing in the whole world could ever either surprise or startle her any more. She felt sure that whatever should come to her in the future would find her ready. She would take the outstretched hand of any new experience and say, "I was expecting you." Her powers seemed to her to have taken up their position upon a level surface and to have lost all ability to rise or fall. The fires had burned too close to have left material to ever flare up again. There was nothing left, she thought, to kindle a sudden or brilliant blaze. She had accepted the thought of a new daughter with a placidity which shocked herself, when she thought of it, until she analyzed her sensations or her lack of them.

The month passed. When the happy young

creatures came, the very beauty of their faces and forms about the house gave warmth and color. Roy was still limping a little and his lung needed care, but he was as handsome as a young fellow could be, and as proud and bright in his new happiness as if the earth were his. "Is she not beautiful?" he would ask twenty times a day, holding the laughing young wife at arm's length. "*Isn't* she beautiful, father?" and Griffith would pretend to turn critical eyes upon her and tease the son with an assumption that it was necessary to look for a beauty which was both rare and graciously, brilliantly endowed.

"Well, let me see! L-e-t—me s-e-e! Turn around, daughter—No, not so far—M-mm. Well—it—seems—to—me—she is r-a-t-h-e-r fair!" and Griffith's eyes would twinkle with pleasure when Emma tweaked his ears or drowned his pretense in a dash of music. The old piano gave place to a new one, and the home was once more filled with laughter and music and a happiness that not even the shadow cast by the thought of the two absent ones could make dark enough to veil the spirits of the two who had come. With the others it had also its infection. So true is it that after long and terrible strains we hail partial relief with such peans of joy that the shadows that remain seem only to temper the light that has burst upon our long darkened vision and to render us only the better able to bear the relief. Griffith sang the old hymns daily now, and even essayed to add his uncertain voice to the gay music that Emma and Roy flung forth.

> "And the nights shall be filled with music,
> And the thoughts that infest the day,
> Shall fold their tents, like the Arabs,
> And as silently steal away."

Emma's voice rang out clear and sweet, and it seemed to Katherine that, after all, it was very delightful to have a new daughter like this one, and if Roy *must* marry, why——

Good news continued to come from the front. Howard and Beverly were well and unhurt. In their different ways they wrote cheerful and cheering letters. Emma grew more radiant every day as she watched the returning color come to Roy's cheeks, and one day Griffith took her by both arms as she was flashing past him. He held her at arm's length and laughed.

"Trying to see if I'm pretty, father?" she said saucily, lifting her mouth for a kiss.

"Pretty! pretty! Why, daughter of Babylon, the lilies of the field are not half so lovely—and Solomon, in all his glory——" He stepped back and folded his arms. Emma flung both little hands up to his cheeks in glee. "Kiss me! oh, you dear old father! Solomon in all his glory never knew you—didn't have you for a father—and so that is where I have got the best of Solomon! Poor old Solomon, I wouldn't trade with him!" She ran laughing down the hall, and Katherine smiled up at her husband.

"What a dear girl she is! I am so glad for Roy—for all of us;" she said. "It is easy and a pleasure to build on an addition to our air-castles for her."

Griffith bent over to kiss her. "Yes, God has been very good to us all the days of our lives, Katherine. The struggles have all been outside of the most sacred—of——" He hesitated as he recalled some of the struggles, and touched his lips to her hair where the gray was growing distinct. "But all those seem to be about over, now, and for us the dawn is here and the brilliant day is only just ahead. Ah, little wife, the sun will rise for us to-morrow on a day which shall have no conflict of soul before us. How happy we shall be when the other boys get home! It makes me feel young again only to think of it! I am going over to the College now. A business meeting of the trustees." He smiled back at her and went humming down the lawn: "Joy to the world, the Lord is come!"

Two hours later in the twilight, there was a confused scuffle of feet and babble of muffled voices on the front porch. Katherine, ever on the alert for news from her absent sons, opened the door. A dark, repellent face—the face of an ascetic, cast in the mold of sorrow and soured by the action of time, was before her. She recognized the pastor of the church near by. "Sister Davenport," he said, "you had better step back. We have sad news. We—— He is dead."

"Which one? Which one?" cried Katherine. "Howard or Beverly?" She was struggling to push by them out on to the porch. Roy rushed from the hallway and past the group.

"Great God! It is father! It is father!" he cried, and turned to shield his mother from the sight. "Come back! Come back!" he said grasping her by the waist and trying to force her into a chair. He had, as we all have at such times, a vague idea of somehow saving her by gaining time. The little group was staggering into the room and its load was laid upon the couch. Griffith Davenport was dead. The smile on the face was there still, but the poor brave heart would beat no more forever.

"Heart failure," some one said, "in the trustees' room."

"In the midst of life we are in death—" began the stern-faced ascetic as he took his place near Katherine. Roy had pushed her into a chair and stood holding her about the shoulders. Emma knelt before her with streaming eyes, looking into the set face. Little Margaret was weeping with fear. She had never before seen the face of death. She did not understand. She only knew that some terrible blow had fallen, and she clung to aunt Judy and wept.

"In the midst of life we are in death. The Lord giveth, and——"

"Oh, go away, go away!" moaned Katherine, as the monotonous voice and the tall form of the clergyman forced itself into her consciousness again. "Go away and leave me with my dead!" She was dry-eyed and staring. She sat like one in a dream. She had not reckoned upon *this* when she had felt that she was ready for anything that should come—anything that could come to her in the future. She was too dazed to grasp or adjust anything now. She only knew that she must be alone. "Go away! go away," she said looking up at Roy. He motioned the men and the minister out and closed and locked the door. When he returned to his mother's side her eyes were shut and her head was thrown back against the chair. There were no tears. He beckoned Judy to bring little Margaret, and he took his mother's arms and put them about the child, and his own were around both. His own eyes were streaming but hers were dry still.

"Mother," he said softly, "mother," She

did not answer. Presently she opened her eyes and they fell upon the child in her arms.

"Poor fatherless child! Poor fatherless child!" she moaned, and the tears gushed forth, but her arms dropped slowly from Margaret's form, and she did not seem to want the child there. The streaming eyes traveled toward the couch and its silent occupant whose trials and struggles were indeed over at last. Oh, the irony of fate! No conflict of soul was before him, the dawn he had heralded—the brilliant day was come, was it not? Who was there to say? He was out of bondage at last—bondage to a conscience and a condition that tortured his brave, sensitive soul. The end of the sacrifice had come, but for what? To Katherine, as she gazed at him lying there in the gloom, it was dead sea-fruit indeed. She could not think. She only sat and stared, and was conscious of the dull dead pain—the worthlessness of all things.

Roy bent down and stroked her hair and kissed her. She did not seem to know. "Shall we go away, too? *All* of us, mother? Would you rather be alone—with father?"

"Yes," she said feebly. "I will be alone always, alone now, always alone—alone!"

"No, no, mother, you will have *all* of us—all—all—but him. We will——"

"Go away! go away, for a while," she said, and flung herself on her knees beside the couch. "Oh, Griffith, Griffith! What was it all for? All our suffering and trials and hopes and life? What was it all for at last?" she moaned with her arms about his lifeless form. "What did it all mean? What was it all for, if *this* is the end? Oh, Griffith, Griffith! what was the use? What was the use—with *this* for the end! I felt so safe about you, darling, now that you were here! I did not even think of you! I did not fear it was you! Oh, Griffith, Griffith! this is the end of all things! This is the end! This is the end! I do not care what else comes—I do not care—I do not care! What is a country? What are sons to *me* now? I do not care! I do not care! This is the end!"

Roy had heard her voice and her sobs. He opened the door softly and saw her with her head on the breast of her dead and the long sobbing sighs coming with the silences between.

He closed the door noiselessly again, and took his young wife in his arms. His voice was choked and broken.

"Emma, my darling, perhaps if you were to go to her—perhaps she would know that *you* can understand—perhaps you could comfort her, if——"

"No, no, Roy, she would hate me if I were to go in there now—I who have you! I who am so happy and so blest! I know! I know, darling. Let her alone—for awhile. Oh, Roy. If it were you! If—if—it were I in there, with—with *you* dead! Oh, Roy!"

They clung to each other in silence. Both understood. At last he said, holding his wife to his heaving breast: "And we cannot help her! Not even God can help her now—if there be a God—not even He can help her now! He would be too late to undo His own cruelty! Ah, love and death! Love and death! how could a good God make both!"

The young wife shuddered and was silent. Her faith could not compass that situation. Love was too new and too strong. Doubt entered the door Love had swung open for these two, and took up his seat at their fireside forever.

An hour later, as they talked in whispers, Roy said: " To think that we all escaped in battle—and he from worse danger—and now! "

" Mos' Roy, honey, I wisht yoh'd take dis heah rabbit foot in dar t' Mis' Kate! Lawsy, Mos' Roy, she gwine ter go outen her mine if she don' look out. Aunt Judy don' need dis heah foot lack what Mis' Kate do now, honey. You des go in dar an' des kinder put hit inter Mis' Kate's pocket er somewheres. Hit ain't gwine ter do her no harhm—an' mebby hit mout do 'er some kine er good, kase I gwine ter *gib* hit to her ter keep fer all de time now."

Roy took the proffered gift quite gravely. " Thank you, aunt Judy, you were always good to us—always. I will take it in there after a while; " he said, and the heroic old soul hobbled away, happy in her supreme sacrifice.

It was night. . . . . To Katherine it seemed that the darkness must be eternal. Yet the sun rose on the morrow, and Life took up its threads and wove on another loom.

THE END.

From the Press of the Arena Publishing Company.

The Rise of the Swiss Republic.
By W. D. McCrackan, A. M.

It contains over four hundred pages, printed from new and handsome type, on a fine quality of heavy paper. The margins are wide, and the volume is richly bound in cloth.

Price, postpaid, $3.00.

Sultan to Sultan.
By M. French-Sheldon (Bebe Bwana).

Being a thrilling account of a remarkable expedition to the Masai and other hostile tribes of East Africa, which was planned and commanded by this intrepid woman. **A Sumptuous Volume of Travels.** Handsomely illustrated; printed on coated paper and richly bound in African red silk-finished cloth.

Price, postpaid, $5.00.

The League of the Iroquois.
By Benjamin Hathaway.

It is instinct with good taste and poetic feeling, affluent of picturesque description and graceful portraiture, and its versification is fairly melodious. — *Harper's Magazine.*

Has the charm of Longfellow's "Hiawatha." — *Albany Evening Journal.*

Of rare excellence and beauty. — *American Wesleyan.*

Evinces fine qualities of imagination, and is distinguished by remarkable grace and fluency. — *Boston Gazette.*

The publication of this poem alone may well serve as a mile-post in marking the pathway of American literature. The work is a marvel of legendary lore, and will be appreciated by every earnest reader. — *Boston Times.*

Price, postpaid, cloth, $1.00; Red Line edition, $1.50.

For sale by all booksellers. Sent postpaid upon receipt of the price.

Arena Publishing Company,
Copley Square,   **BOSTON, MASS.**

From the Press of the Arena Publishing Company.

Is This Your Son, My Lord?

By HELEN H. GARDENER. The most powerful novel written by an American. A terrible *expose* of conventional immorality and hypocrisy. Price: paper, 50 cents; cloth, $1.00.

Pray You, Sir, Whose Daughter?

By HELEN H. GARDENER. A brilliant novel of to-day, dealing with social purity and the "age of consent" laws. Price: paper, 50 cents; cloth, $1.00.

A Spoil of Office.

A novel. By HAMLIN GARLAND. The truest picture of Western life that has appeared in American fiction. Price: paper, 50 cents; cloth, $1.00.

Lessons Learned from Other Lives.

By B. O. FLOWER.

There are fourteen biographies in this volume, dealing with the lives of Seneca and Epictetus, the great Roman philosophers; Joan of Arc, the warrior maid; Henry Clay, the statesman; Edwin Booth and Joseph Jefferson, the actors; John Howard Payne, William Cullen Bryant, Edgar Allan Poe, Alice and Phœbe Cary, and John G. Whittier, the poets; Alfred Russell Wallace, the scientist; Victor Hugo, the many-sided man of genius.

"The book sparkles with literary jewels." — *Christian Leader*, Cincinnati, Ohio.

Price: paper, 50 cents; cloth. $1.00.

For sale by all booksellers. Sent postpaid upon receipt of the price.

Arena Publishing Company,

Copley Square,   BOSTON, MASS.

BOOKS

From the Press of the Arena Publishing Company.

Along Shore with a Man of War.

By MARGUERITE DICKINS. A delightful story of travel, delightfully told, handsomely illustrated, and beautifully bound. Price, postpaid, $1.50.

Evolution.

Popular lectures by leading thinkers, delivered before the Brooklyn Ethical Association. This work is of inestimable value to the general reader who is interested in Evolution as applied to religious, scientific, and social themes. It is the joint work of a number of the foremost thinkers in America to-day. One volume, handsome cloth, illustrated, complete index. 408 pp. Price, postpaid, $2.00.

Sociology.

Popular lectures by eminent thinkers, delivered before the Brooklyn Ethical Association. This work is a companion volume to "Evolution," and presents the best thought of representative thinkers on social evolution. One volume, handsome cloth, with diagram and complete index. 412 pp. Price, postpaid, $2.00.

For sale by all booksellers. Sent postpaid upon receipt of the price.

Arena Publishing Company,

Copley Square,   BOSTON, MASS.

From the Press of the Arena Publishing Company.

Songs.

By NEITH BOYCE. Illustrated with original drawings by ETHELWYN WELLS CONREY. A beautiful gift book. Bound in white and gold. Price, postpaid, $1.25.

The Finished Creation, and Other Poems.

By BENJAMIN HATHAWAY, author of "The League of the Iroquois," "Art Life," and other Poems. Handsomely bound in white parchment vellum, stamped in silver. Price, postpaid, $1.25.

Wit and Humor of the Bible.

By Rev. MARION D. SHUTTER, D.D. A brilliant and reverent treatise. Published only in cloth. Price, postpaid, $1.50.

Son of Man; or, Sequel to Evolution.

By CELESTIA ROOT LANG. Published only in cloth.

This work, in many respects, very remarkably discusses the next step in the Evolution of Man. It is in perfect touch with advanced Christian Evolutionary thought, but takes a step beyond the present position of Religion Leaders.

Price, postpaid, $1.25.

For sale by all booksellers. Sent postpaid upon receipt of the price.

Arena Publishing Company,

Copley Square,   BOSTON, MASS.

From the Press of the Arena Publishing Company.

The Dream Child.
A fascinating romance of two worlds. By FLORENCE HUNTLEY. Price: paper, 50 cents; cloth, $1.00.

A Mute Confessor.
The romance of a Southern town. By WILL N. HARBEN, author of "White Marie," "Almost Persuaded," etc. Price: paper, 50 cents; cloth, $1.00.

Redbank; Life on a Southern Plantation.
By M. L. COWLES. A typical Southern story by a Southern woman. Price: paper, 00; cloth, $1.00.

Psychics. Facts and Theories.
By Rev. MINOT J. SAVAGE. A thoughtful discussion of Psychical problems. Price: paper, 50 cents; cloth, $1.00.

Civilization's Inferno: Studies in the Social Cellar.
By B. O. FLOWER. I. Introductory chapter. II. Society's Exiles. III. Two Hours in the Social Cellar. IV. The Democracy of Darkness. V. Why the Ishmaelites Multiply. VI. The Froth and the Dregs. VII. A Pilgrimage and a Vision. VIII. Some Facts and a Question. IX. What of the Morrow? Price: paper, 50 cents; cloth, $1.00.

For sale by all booksellers. Sent postpaid upon receipt of the price.

Arena Publishing Company,

Copley Square,   **BOSTON, MASS.**

From the Press of the Arena Publishing Company.

Jason Edwards: An Average Man.

By HAMLIN GARLAND. A powerful and realistic story of to-day. Price: paper, 50 cents; cloth, $1.00.

Who Lies? An Interrogation.

By BLUM and ALEXANDER. A book that is well worth reading. Price: paper, 50 cents; cloth, $1.00.

Main Travelled Roads.

Six Mississippi Valley stories. By HAMLIN GARLAND.

"The sturdy spirit of true democracy runs through this book." — *Review of Reviews.*

Price: paper, 50 cents; cloth, $1.00.

Irrepressible Conflict Between Two World-Theories.

By Rev. MINOT J. SAVAGE. The most powerful presentation of Theistic Evolution *versus* Orthodoxy that has ever appeared. Price: paper, 50 cents; cloth, $1.00.

For sale by all booksellers. Sent postpaid upon receipt of the price.

Arena Publishing Company,

Copley Square,   BOSTON, MASS.

From the Press of the Arena Publishing Company.

Salome Shepard, Reformer.

By HELEN M. WINSLOW. A New England story. Price. paper, 50 cents; cloth, $1.00.

The Law of Laws.

By S. B. WAIT. The author takes advance metaphysical grounds on the origin, nature, and destiny of the soul.

"It is offered as a contribution to the thought of that unnumbered fraternity of spirit whose members are found wherever souls are sensitive to the impact of the truth and feel another's burden as their own."— *Author's Preface.*

256 pages; handsome cloth. Price, postpaid, $1.50.

Life. A Novel.

By WILLIAM W. WHEELER. A book of thrilling interest from cover to cover.

In the form of a novel called "LIFE," William W. Wheeler has put before the public some of the clearest statements of logical ideas regarding humanity's present aspects, its inherent and manifest powers, and its future, that we have ever read. The book is strong, keen, powerful; running over with thought, so expressed as to clearly convey the author's ideas; everything is to the point, nothing superfluous — and for this it is specially admirable. — *The Boston Times.*

Price: paper, 50 cents; cloth, $1.00.

For sale by all booksellers. Sent postpaid upon receipt of the price.

Arena Publishing Company,

Copley Square,   BOSTON, MASS.

∴ *From the Press of the Arena Publishing Company.* ∴

CIVILIZATION'S INFERNO.

STUDIES IN THE SOCIAL CELLAR.

BY B. O. FLOWER.

A bold, unconventional book which in a merciless manner lays bare the criminal extravagance, the disgusting flunkyism, and the immorality found in what the author terms the "Froth of Society."

It fearlessly contrasts the criminal extravagance and moral effeminacy of the slothful rich with the terrible social, moral, and physical condition of the ignorant, starving, and degraded poor.

It carries the reader into the social cellar where uninvited poverty abounds, and from there into the sub-cellar, or the world of the criminal poor.

It is rich in suggestive hints, and should be in the hands of every thoughtful man and woman in America.

TABLE OF CONTENTS.— I. Introductory Chapter. II. Society's Exiles. III. Two Hours in the Social Cellar. IV. The Democracy of Darkness. V. Why the Ishmaelites Multiply. VI. The Froth and the Dregs. VII. A Pilgrimage and a Vision. VIII. What of the Morrow.

Price: paper, 50 cents; cloth, $1.25.

PRESS COMMENTS.

It is a strong appeal to the Christian civilization of the times to arise and change the current of human misery which in these modern times is driving with such resistless force.—*Chicago Daily Inter-Ocean.*

A thoughtful work by a thoughtful man, and should turn the minds of many who are now ignorant or careless to the condition of the countless thousands who live in the "social cellar."— *Courier-Journal, Louisville, Ky.*

Society, as it is now constituted, is nothing less than a sleeping volcano. Who dares to say how soon the upheaval will come, or whether it can be evaded by the adoption of prompt measures of relief? Certainly the condition of the lower social strata calls for immediate action on the part of those whose safety is at stake. Mr. Flower has accomplished a great work, in setting forth the exact truth of the matter, without any effort at palliation.—*Boston Beacon.*

For sale by all booksellers. *Sent post-paid upon receipt of the price.*

Arena Publishing Company,

Copley Square,   Boston, Mass.

BOOKS

∴ *From the press of the Arena Publishing Company.* ∴

SIDE POCKET SERIES.

A GUIDE TO PALMISTRY.

By E. J. E. HENDERSON. One of the most interesting and charming books of the year. The hand is a perfect indicator of character. This book gives you the key. Handsomely illustrated. *Price, cloth, 75 cents.*

THE OPEN SECRET.

By A. PRIEST. A message from Mars. The secret of life and destiny. A unique and intensely interesting book. Illustrated with head and tail pieces. *Price, cloth, 75 cents.*

DR. JOHN SAWYER.

By MRS. ELVINA J. BARTLETT. A beautiful and interesting story. Illustrated with head and tail pieces. *Price, cloth, 75 cents.*

ONE DAY. A Tale of the Prairies.

By ELBERT HUBBARD. A most interesting book. The chapters are: I. Morning. II. Noon. III. Afternoon. IV. Night. Illustrated with beautiful original designs. The first and last chapters show drawings in miniature of Michael Angelo's "Morning" and "Night," from the figures on the tomb of Lorenzo de Medici, at Florence. *Price, cloth, 75 cents.*

For sale by all booksellers.   Sent post-paid upon receipt of the price.

Arena Publishing Company,

Copley Square,   Boston, Mass.

BOOKS

∴ *From the press of the Arena Publishing Company.* ∴

ALBERT BRISBANE.

A Mental Biography, with a Character Study.

By his wife, Redelia Brisbane.

One handsome volume. Cloth. 365 pages. Price, $2.00.

This work, in the form of an autobiographical recital, covers many of the most important events of the century. In this splendid book will be found subjects of the most varied character. Mr. Brisbane's unique experience as a student, a traveller, and a philosophic observer, together with his rare power of original thought, invests with peculiar interest every subject touched upon, — prominent among which is a vivid picture of the social movement from the days of St. Simon down to the present.

ECCE ORATOR!

CHRIST THE ORATOR;

or, Never Man Spake Like This Man.

By Rev. T. ALEXANDER HYDE. A book that will have a million readers since it fills a most important and long time vacant niche in the temple of literature. It is in many ways the most brilliant and most remarkable treatise of the age, for it is a masterly and complete exposition of a subject almost untouched by any writer, and by its thorough investigation and original thought renders topics long veiled in night as clear as noonday.

Though profoundly scholarly, yet the style is so fascinating that it is as interesting as a romance. Like a brilliant electric search light it casts its effulgence along the hills of Palestine and reveals the Christ in wonderful reality. Not until you have read this book have you seen the real Christ as He walked the valleys of Judea and preached to vast assemblies His world-wide truths. Price, cloth, $1.25.

For sale by all booksellers.   *Sent post-paid upon receipt of the price.*

Arena Publishing Company,

Copley Square,   Boston, Mass.

www.ingramcontent.com/pod-product-compliance
Lightning Source LLC
Chambersburg PA
CBHW031422230426
43668CB00007B/403